I DON'T HAVE A BUCKET LIST BUT MY F*CK-IT LIST IS A MILE LONG

RUBY REY

Disclaimer:

This book is for entertainment purposes only.

Ruby Rey is not a doctor, lawyer, accountant, baker, or candlestick maker.

All views in this literary masterpiece are the opinions of the author, and should be taken with a grain of salt, a lick of lime, and a shot of tequila.

DEARLY BELOVED

Nobody went to my great-grandfather's funeral.

You might be thinking my great-grandfather was a terrible man, perhaps a war criminal, or a mean drunk, or a serial abuser. He wasn't. The old fellow was simply a bitter grouch who had no use for others, unless they were of use to him. He cashed in his chips at the ripe old age of 92, long after his contemporaries had passed, but even if he'd died decades sooner, the seats in the chapel would have been empty.

Bummer, right? Stick with me. There are two good reasons I'm telling you this story.

First, now you are thinking about your own funeral. As soon as I mentioned the word funeral, you went there. It's a natural leap. We all wonder how we measure up to others. Some people say the funeral is the final score card for your life.

Hey! I've got a fun idea. Let's go there now. Let's jump into your imagination and have a peek at your funeral.

Is it a small, intimate affair? Who's there? A handful of people who truly knew and loved you?

Are they smiling as they wipe a tear from their eyes? Is someone saying, "The ol' gal sure knew how to live life on her own terms!" or "Hey, has anyone given her a poke to make sure she's really dead?"

Or maybe it's a big funeral. If you're a famous muck-a-muck, even your pickled corpse will pull a crowd. If you're a member of a large organization, all the other members are obligated to attend. You will get the numbers, even if a third of these so-called grievers are checking their phones during the eulogy. After the hymns, the phone-checkers will make a bee-line for the sandwich trays, and their carefree laughter will punctuate the family's grief in that absurd way of funerals.

In this imaginary scenario, are you survived by a sturdy spouse with a few miles left on him? If so, your funeral will attract overly-made-up, sun-damaged-cleavage-flaunting widower hunters on the prowl. The hussies! Look at them, eating the crustless egg salad sandwiches you paid for while slipping your husband their phone number with an invitation to call, any time of day or night, "just to talk."

And, oh, the expense of it all! Big or small, funerals aren't cheap.

Now unclench your fists, let out a sigh, and push away all thoughts of death.

How did that mental exercise make you feel? Not good, right?

If picturing your funeral made you feel lousy, it's not your fault. It's mine. I know perfectly well that nobody enjoys that mental exercise. Nobody. It's a mean trick that supposedly wise people use to make themselves seem smarter and holier than you.

Total dick move on my part.

As my way of making amends, I pledge to you that the rest of this book contains nothing designed to make you feel bad, or unworthy, or like you are *not enough*.

You, dearly beloved, are wonderful and unique, and you absolutely *are* enough, no matter the size of your social footprint. You have so much good inside you that you can't even imagine it. Your capacity for love is bigger than your outstretched arms, and brighter than the sun.

What if, starting now, you put that tired exercise of imagining your funeral right where it belongs?

ON YOUR FUCK-IT LIST.

Along with all the other silly things you don't have to do anymore.

A funeral is not the score card for a life.

My great-grandfather lived life on his own terms, exactly like someone who didn't care who came to his funeral. I can't say I agree with all his choices, such as giving my great-grandmother syphilis he caught from the slutty mail carrier, but his life was what it was. His score card was known to all long before his funeral.

You, on the other hand, haven't given my ancestors any sexually transmitted infections (that I know of), so that would technically give you a point on him. Unless you commit some heinous crimes before you shuffle off, you're guaranteed to have more attendees at your funeral than he did. Regardless, let's not keep score. Your life can't be compared to my great-grandfather's any more than it can be compared to anyone else's.

Repeat after me: *My funeral is not the score card for my life.*

The next time someone tells you to imagine your own funeral, imagine yourself instead eating a delicious egg salad sandwich at *their* funeral.

* * *

The second reason I brought up my great-grandfather's unattended funeral is because the man was an asshole. And he wasn't the only one in the family tree.

Like many people who are drawn into comedy, I come from a long, unbroken line of assholes, going all the way back to Adam and Eve's shittiest offspring. (Note to my religious friends: That is the one and only bible reference in this book, but there will be more cursing.)

It's not easy to grow up and become good, or kind, or happy without the DNA. It's doubly hard when you don't have the role models. Being born of assholes and raised by assholes, I had a lot of obstacles to overcome.

Spoiler alert: I am currently a happy and productive member of society. (If you generously consider being a comedy writer *productive*.)

I now have what people in the lucrative self-help industry call Abundance with a Capital A: good friends, money, a trim figure, and a handsome husband who assures people all the time that he is not being held captive.

Because I have more than enough, I'd love to share what I've learned. If I tell you all my tips, and tricks, and life hacks, and shortcuts, and secret handshakes, will you promise to come to my funeral?

Just kidding. I don't give a shit who comes to my funeral. And neither should you.

But I will tell you everything I know about how to roll with life's punches and keep laughing as you get richer, happier, and kick-ass-ier.

Note to editor: Yes, kick-ass-ier is a word!

NAKED OLD MEN
RIDING BICYCLES

Have you ever tried to help someone, only to have it backfire?

What's that old saying?

No good deed goes unpunished.

First you do the right thing, then you get a kick up the backside. Not every single time, but enough to be discouraging.

Let's say you inform your spouse they're loading the dishwasher incorrectly. The chances of them becoming snippy, passive aggressive, or downright hostile are approximately 100%.

Let's say you do what you believe is the right thing and inform a close friend about their partner's infidelity. The chances of your friend screaming at you that you've always been envious of them, you jealous hater, and then burning down your house are approximately 100%.

Nobody likes having their mistakes pointed out. The maker of the mistakes will attempt to erase all evidence, even going so far as to get rid of those who remind them of their failures. Humiliation and shame are powerful motivators.

Hurt people hurt people, as the saying goes, and these hurt people will do anything to ease their pain by spreading the blame.

If, like me, you are a reasonably clever person, you will have ample opportunities to deliver relationship-destroying advice to everyone you know. But if you are as wise as you are clever, you will keep this wisdom to yourself.

What if you still want to help others? How sweet. I love your good heart. There is a way, and I'll share it with you now.

The most ingenious way to help others is to be... ever so slightly smug.

What I mean by *ever so slightly smug* is that you must smile knowingly while casually leading by example. The safety videos on airlines advise that, in the event of cabin depressurization, you should put on your own oxygen mask before helping others with theirs. The same logic applies to all aspects of life. To help others, first help yourself. If you ever feel the urge to dispense unsolicited advice, bite your tongue. Get back to work on yourself.

While you are working on leveling up to Boss levels, you must never talk about what you're doing. In fact, do the opposite. Act like it's a secret. Nobody can resist a secret.

Become a Boss quietly, sneakily, and soon everyone will be *begging* for your advice. When asked, let out a few of your *secrets* begrudgingly. Let your friend or family member think it's their idea. When their eyes glaze over, stop talking immediately. Change takes time. To the closed mind, all wisdom sounds like nonsense.

Keep at it.

Even the act of you reading this book is helping others. Every life upgrade you make will ripple outward exponentially, but only if you act nonchalant. Not fully smug, but *ever so slightly* smug. Accept your many incoming compliments with an enigmatic Mona Lisa smile.

Note: Choose your battles wisely. No amount of nonchalance will win over a stubborn person when it comes to loading the dishwasher. That particular kitchen appliance, and the care and feeding of said appliance, is a no-win zone.

* * *

You probably noticed there's a swear word on the cover of this book. If you guessed that something titled *I Don't Have a Bucket List But my Fuck-It List is a Mile Long* won't take itself too seriously, DING DING, we have a winner!

When I started writing this book, I didn't want the universe to give me a kick in the ass for trying to *help* people. That's why I focused on having fun, helping myself. And it worked. I have had far more fun and gained much more insight than I dared hope for.

While this chapter appears near the front of the book, I have actually written these words toward the end of the process. This is Ruby Rey from the future.

Hello.

I'm the Ruby Rey who has finished this labor of love, her very first funny self-help memoir. This Ruby Rey has been on a journey of self discovery and growth, exactly like that lady in *Eat Pray Love*, except without taking off my sweatpants. Or traveling to other countries. Or meditating.

Okay, so my process was probably nothing like Elizabeth Gilbert's, but in my defense, I've never actually read that book. A friend gave me a copy for Christmas, so naturally I rejected it the way I would reject any unsolicited advice given by others.

But, like Elizabeth Gilbert, whom I have heard speak about creativity in general, I have been willing to dive deep in order to learn and share. By recalling the most awkward moments of my life, I got to remember so many sweet and funny details that would have otherwise been lost to time. By searching for the lessons I've learned, I gained meaningful perspective and, dare I say it, wisdom.

At one point during the writing of this book, I confessed breathlessly to a friend, "I feel like I'm falling in love with myself."

My friend rolled her eyes so hard she banged her head on the wall. It still makes me giggle. What are friends for if not for laughing with you?

With this book, that's what I want to be. A friend who laughs with you—not *at* you—and gives you perspective.

I'm not trying to "help" you, because you're already doing the best you can. All I can do is tell the truth—the truth according to Ruby Rey. You can take my truth and do whatever you want with it. You can burn, erase, or delete this book. Or you can write your favorite quotes on Post-It notes and put them on your bathroom mirror, where my wisdom will catch the chunks that fly out of your teeth during flossing. Whatever you get out of this book is your business.

By the powers vested in me, I hereby give you permission to relax and enjoy this book. There's no quiz at the end. You will not be graded. You are under no obligation to suddenly become a completely different, new and improved person. Phew.

Think of me as the sassy girlfriend who's in every romantic comedy. The goofy one with the curly hair who assures the main character that she's perfect, except for maybe one or two blind spots—nothing that can't be solved with a pep talk, a makeover, and a shot of tequila slurped out of Channing Tatum's belly button.

As I write these words, I'm forty-four years old. The candles on my last birthday cake set off the smoke detector. Forty-four is just old enough to have learned some stuff, and just young enough to remember what it was like to not know that stuff.

Nobody asked me to write this book, but I started anyway. If you sit around waiting for someone to ask you what you think, you'll be waiting a long damn time. I know this fact because I am forty-four big ones. Behold my birthday cake, and all my flaming torches of wisdom.

Every anecdote in this book is completely true. I've made a few adjustments for simplicity's sake. For example, a couple of similar people have been merged together, like Frankenstein's monster. I've changed names and identifying details to protect the innocent and the guilty, as well as myself from being sued.

In my endeavor to hold nothing back, I may go too far. If I deeply offend you in any way, I do apologize.

Comedy has always been tough. Comedy writers struggle to find the balance between providing entertainment and getting sacked from our jobs.

Comedy is like acupuncture—that treatment where you're poked with very fine needles. The idea is that your body responds to a therapeutic amount of damage by getting to work repairing itself. The treatment gives you better immunity, lowers your stress hormones, and improves your overall health.

The way I see it, a joke that stings is like an acupuncture needle being poked directly into your ego. If a joke feels uncomfortable, it may have been told in poor taste, or it could be a sign your ego needs more poking. Get yourself poked. If further poking causes hot air to leak out, well, consider yourself on the path to healing that most terrible of afflictions: self importance.

Humor is underrated. The Oscar award for Best Picture rarely goes to a comedy. Scholarships aren't awarded to the class clown. Boys don't fight over the girl with the funny glasses. So, if your sense of humor isn't as robust as you'd like it to be, blame society.

If you find yourself losing your sense of humor, take it as seriously as you would a fever, a lump, or a purple rash on your neck that looks an awful lot like the number 666. Get it treated before it worsens.

The best treatment for a lack of laughter is to adopt a shelter pet. The second best treatment is to spend time with people who make you laugh, either in person or through your favorite movies, TV shows, comedy specials, live theater, podcasts, books, and so forth.

Short doses of humor are everywhere. If you're in a store with a greeting card display, read the jokes inside the cards that have black and white pictures of naked old men on bicycles. In fact, any time of day or night, you can always think about naked old men riding bicycles. Those droopy wrinkles! The buttcrack resting on the puny little seat! It's a guaranteed mood booster.

That fun tip is just one of many secrets in store for you. Want to be popular at parties and have more confidence? Keep reading. You'll learn how to trick yourself into having better habits, deal with frenemies and false teachers, plus how and why you should become a community leader. Get ready to sidestep the three big pitfalls on the path to true happiness. Take note of my unique marriage tips, and you won't want to miss my one weird trick for preventing bad days, as well as...

Wait.

Why am I telling you what's in store?

By the time you finish reading *I Don't Have a Bucket List But My Fuck-It List is a Mile Long*, you will have forgotten all of the bold promises I've made in these early chapters.

So let's get to it.

PRACTICE SAFE SNIPING

If I am out of the house at some event, and I send an email or text message to a friend to report on the event, I refrain from making any criticism. Even if the event is a total shit show, I do not say so in my message.

I do this because there's always a possibility I might die before I make it back home to my house. I would hate for my next of kin to discover that my last words were nasty ones. Also, as we all know from books and movies, sending such messages creates bad karma in the form of ironic coincidence.

"Ruby Rey's final words, as texted to an acquaintance, were, 'This community theater play is hot garbage.' That's our Ruby! She always thought everything was hot garbage. It's such an irony that, on her way home from the play, she was tragically run over by a dump truck full of hot garbage."

COCOON

The summer of 1985 is a good one for movies, even in a small town with only a single screen. I eat wine gums and watch, for the first time, movies that I will rewatch many times over the coming years. These films include such classics as *The Goonies*, *Back to the Future*, *Gremlins*, and *National Lampoon's European Vacation*.

I also waste some allowance money seeing *Cocoon*. I will never watch *Cocoon* again, except for by accident while flipping through TV channels. Seeing it this way is inevitable, because, by law, *Cocoon* is continuously playing on at least three cable channels at all times. *Cocoon* is a movie about senior citizens swimming with giant clams. There's a sequel, *Cocoon: The Return*, in which the giant clams rampage through New York until they're beaten back by Tom Hanks and his big-dicked sidekick, John Candy. Or so I imagine, since I haven't seen it. I may be mixing it up with *Splash*.

Summer ends and it's September.

Back to school!

(We're in a flashback anecdote right now, in case you haven't noticed my use of present tense.)

I'm eleven years old. I'm a Capricorn, born at the tail end of the year, so while most eleven-year-olds are entering sixth grade, I'm heading for the seventh. In my hometown, elementary school goes from kindergarten to grade seven. It's my last year here before I move on to junior high.

This morning, I'm excited as I get dressed. I've carefully chosen my outfit, which came from K-Mart, as do all my clothes. My pants are what will be called, in the future, Mom Jeans. For now, they're just jeans. I pair them with a new sweatshirt, which is as bright and white as a Tide commercial, with batwing sleeves and a cat on the front. Except it's not really a cat. It's the airbrushed rendering of a cat's eyes, nose, and whiskers. You have to imagine the rest of the cat. These shirts come in white or black, which makes sense, but also pink, which doesn't make sense.

Over a breakfast of shredded wheat and milk, my mother gives me the usual speech about how time will pass more quickly as I get closer to her age, until it's whipping by in a frenzy. Her tone is ominous, vengeful.

In the front yard, I pose with my siblings for the annual first-day-of-school photo, then we're off. I climb into the car carefully, holding my arms close to my sides so that the grimy interior of our old vehicle doesn't smudge my sweatshirt.

The radio plays "The Power of Love," by Huey Lewis and the News. This gives me a pleasant flashback to *Back to the Future*. That young fellow,

Michael J. Fox, certainly is popular! He's also in *Teen Wolf*, which I didn't see.

Next up is a catchy tune by a young lady with one name: Madonna. She is only three years older than Michael J. Fox, but she is a different kind of famous. The media loves Michael J. Fox because both children and adults love Michael J. Fox. Madonna, however, is terrifying. My father will talk about Michael J. Fox over dinner, but whenever the topic of Madonna comes up, he pretends to not know who that is. It must be her lace gloves, not the fact she's a sexual female with agency. But I digress.

I arrive at school, and it smells like school: industrial cleaners, carpet glue, and damp paper towels. The wall displays in the hallways are bare. I see the new first graders, and, boy oh boy, are they small. *That used to be me*, I think to myself in that old and worldly way that seventh graders have.

I'm bouncing on the balls of my feet as I enter the classroom. I feel so good about myself that it takes several minutes to realize something is wrong.

My jeans are dark blue. Nobody else is wearing dark blue jeans, except for the teacher, who sees me and smiles. "Nice jeans, Ruby!"

I am paralyzed with horror. The teacher likes my jeans? Kill me now.

I take my seat, looking around furtively. The popular girls must have gone shopping together. They're as coordinated as an Olympic team. They wear layers of bright pastels, decorated not with cat whiskers but with brand names. Brand names not sold at K-Mart. I squirm, sweating in my uncool dark jeans. The other girls have matching hair. Spiral perms with straight bangs that have been teased and hair-sprayed and... Uh...

* RECORD SCRATCH SOUND *

Hey, sorry to be interrupt, but can we pop out of this flashback for a minute?

Whoosh!

Back to the present.

You probably noticed this flashback feels familiar, whether you grew up in the 80s or not. This particular pre-teen horror, arriving at school in the wrong clothes, is a total cliché. It's a common trope found in coming-of-age movies, TV series, books, and graphic novels. The fashions vary slightly based on the year, but you've seen this story countless times, and it goes like this:

Kid is excited about their special clothes for the first day back at school. Kid arrives at school only to discover their clothes are tragically uncool. The sequence climaxes with the teenager being humiliated in a contrived situation involving nudity and the school bully and/or the most popular cheerleader.

Why do you suppose these fashion-victim anecdotes are included in so many of our coming-of-age narratives? Is arriving at school in the wrong jeans a thing that happened to all of us and is thus universal and unavoidable? Or are all writers lazy and unimaginative, using existing stories as templates and changing a few details to pretend it's original? Or do we self-anointed outsiders use this particular story because we prefer blaming our peers and the fickleness of fashion for our inability to fit in?

It's much more comfortable for me to blame K-Mart or my mother's cheapness than to admit that the real reason other kids didn't like me was actually my own fault. It was because, deep down, *I didn't like them, either.*

You can't expect people to like you if you don't like them.

And how could I like those other seventh graders? They were just kids, barely above animals; I was a *person*. I had a rich inner life. I had a vocabulary. I was *me*, and they were not, the poor savages.

The ugly truth about outsiders is we are the ones to blame for our situation.

We choose to stand outside.

I'm not saying it's the right choice, let alone a good way to be, but it seems we choose to distance ourselves from others because we outsiders feel, on some level, that we're better than everyone else.

* * *

Now that I take a good, hard look at my first-day-of-school story, the memory is not very solid. As I pick at the details, everything comes apart. It was my sister who had the cat-faced sweatshirt, not me. My flashback unravels, just like an ugly sweater from the 80s.

While the emotional truth is accurate—I did feel out of sync with the other kids—many of the details were, in fact, fabricated. This first-day-of-school narrative I've been telling myself is just a mashup from countless coming-of-age movies. It's like one of those implanted dreams from *Inception*.

My bad.

Now for the real story.

I think what *actually* happened on my first day of seventh grade is that I went to school, continued to believe my clothes were fine, and continued to have no friends, exactly as expected. No punchline. No lessons learned or hugs received.

That means I need to keep digging, because this book needs a youthful flashback like those Antarean aliens in *Cocoon* need their magic swimming pool.

I do have another memory to share. I'm sure it's real because nobody would put this one in a movie except maybe writer-director Harmony Korine, who would make it super gross.

Once again, it's the summer of 1985.

Out of the blue, a popular girl named Sam phones me up and invites me to her house. Sam never paid any attention to me in sixth grade, but now this?

I've always wanted a best friend, or, really, any level of friend.

Now Sam has phoned, and it's happening! This shall be my metamorphosis. I've been a gross caterpillar, but now I'm going to transform into a butterfly.

The next day, I am hopeful and curious when I get dropped off at Sam's house.

An hour into hanging out, things are going well. I make a few jokes, and she tells me I am funny. Funny! At last, someone who appreciates me. I am well on my way to having a best friend. We can get one of those gold necklace charms you break into two halves.

Sam asks why she never noticed how interesting I am. Cut to me, shrugging. Cut back to Sam, tucking her strawberry blonde hair behind her ear and saying it's a shame we didn't become friends sooner. Sadly, she will be moving away before September. That means that when school starts in the fall, I still won't have a friend in my class.

My young heart breaks. I swallow hard and agree that it is a shame.

Then she says, "Let's take off all our clothes and jump naked on the trampoline!"

How can I say no to the girl who is, at that moment, my very best friend in the whole world? It is the first time someone has flattered me into getting naked, but it won't be the last. I begin stripping.

Her body is pale and skinny like mine, all corners and straight lines. Giggling, we compare the color of our skin and the shape of our chests. We are both as flat as boys on top. We fling our clothes off the trampoline and jump as high as we can. I love that moment of stillness at the height of a jump, between rising and falling. It's like the whole world is on pause, ever so briefly. As we jump, Sam and I laugh hysterically over who can swallow air and then burp the loudest.

We are as naked and innocent as newborn angels. Sam's strawberry blonde hair fans out from her head, looking like golden snakes and smelling faintly of her house, which smells like onion soup.

After this, I never see Sam again. Her family moves away before September. That's why this book doesn't contain a story about our first sleepover, in which Sam invites me to smell her fingers.

I still think about her, and how different my life might have been if she hadn't moved away.

How different my life would have been with a childhood best friend.

The idea makes me feel weightless and giddy, like a naked angel paused high in the air above a trampoline.

BUTTERFACE

I'm at a business meeting with other adults.

We've finished with the major stuff and are shooting the breeze about funny pet stories, as people do. I notice that everyone seated at the round table has turned to face the same direction. They resemble a field of sunflowers, tilted to take in the sun. But there is no sun, just a woman.

She sits next to me. She is young, and blonde, and beautiful. She is also kind, well-spoken, and successful.

She makes a joke.

Everyone laughs for seven full minutes.

I, who have equal importance at this meeting, make an equally funny joke.

Zero laughs. Everyone furrows their brows and drops their gazes down to their laps.

I try another comment. No change. My stomach curdles.

Then Little Miss Sunshine speaks again.

Once more, all of their sunflower faces tilt up expectantly. Before she's even finished speaking, the gang is chuckling again.

Something is happening, I think. *I am losing my mind. I'm too young to lose my mind!*

I wait until there's a lull in the conversation before I try speaking again.

This is not the time for risk, so I don't make a joke. I tentatively offer a positive, supportive comment.

Everyone frowns and looks down again. They're embarrassed. You would think I said, "Hey, poopy buttholes, does anyone know if hemorrhoids can spread over to your meatflaps? I may need to see a doctor."

I didn't say anything like that. But feel free to use that line in your own future business meetings to liven the mood!

Little Miss Sunshine spoke again, and everyone at the table was visibly relieved.

I shut my mouth and silently stewed.

It wasn't until I got home and caught a glimpse of myself in the mirror that I figured out what had happened.

No, I didn't have a huge zit on the tip of my nose or a chunk of kale between my teeth. Everything about my face was the same as usual, and that, my dear, was the problem.

I am the type of girl who is euphemistically referred to as *plain*.

I have... a face for radio.

Even today, after two rounds with the plastic surgeon's knife, I am still what's called a Butterface. You know the old joke. Great legs, *but her face*!

* * *

I wasn't always ugly.

Once upon a time I was a beautiful, mysterious loner.

Let's flash back to the 80s again. This is our final trip to the post-polyester, all-cotton decade, so enjoy the slouch socks, legwarmers, and neon hair scrunchies while you can.

The camera pans over to our beautiful, mysterious loner. She is an eleven-year-old girl, sitting alone on the swingset with a book in her hands. Still friendless, a young Ruby Rey has found solace in a fictional world.

Books are much easier than friends. On Friday afternoons, I visit the library and load several into my backpack to take home for a weekend-long sleepover. You can't do that with human children.

As young Ruby kicks the dusty dirt beneath the swing, she flips another page, hoping to finish the chapter before the bell signals the end of recess.

My reading choice is not one of the "problem" books popular in the 80s—the ones about tough, wise-beyond-their-years kids whose parents beat them black and blue in between drug and alcohol binges. I don't care for those books. I find no comfort in imagining lives that are worse than mine.

What I do love to read—what I can't get enough of—are books about kids who discover a strange, giant egg which hatches into a magnificent psychic dragon that becomes the child's new best friend forever and ever. Luckily for me, there are over one million of these books. It is law that for every non-dragon book published there must also be two published about children finding dragon eggs.

If there's a girl in these books, she is always beautiful, though she doesn't realize it until her magnificent psychic dragon points it out. When I read the inner thoughts and powerful emotions felt by these book heroines, these outcasts and orphans, I recognize my own emotions. They feel how I feel. Lost and alone. I am just like them. Therefore, I am also a mysterious, beautiful outcast waiting for her dragon egg.

The bell rings and recess ends. Back to boring school lessons that are too easy for me to be interesting.

And back to the classroom, where another student, a girl who is not having such an easy time with the lessons, lashes out by telling me I'm ugly. Her friends all agree. I may be the smartest girl in the class, but I'm also the ugliest.

This is news to me. I don't want to believe it, but the others seemed so certain. I give it some serious consideration. If I'm ugly, that would explain why nobody wants to be my friend.

When I get home, I look in the bathroom mirror. All I see is myself. I wonder, where is the ugliness? Can it be isolated to one area?

I get a smaller, hand-held mirror that frames one part of my face at a time. I start from the top. My hair can't be the problem. Every hairdresser who's ever touched my head has told me my hair is wonderful, and that people pay good money to get their hair permed to be as curly as mine.

Next, I examine my forehead. I'm still a few years from puberty, so there's no acne yet. Can a forehead be ugly? I don't have a horn or a third eye in the middle of mine, so I guess it's okay.

I tilt the mirror down. My eyes are halfway between green and blue, with a ring of amber. They're the sort of special, lovingly-described eyes that all mysterious, beautiful characters in fantasy novels have. No problem there.

Now we reach my nose. Stop! Loud horn blast! Folks, we have located the source of the problem. Scanning ahead, my lips are a bit thin and my chin is too pointy, but the nose is Enemy Number One. It's bigger than it needs to be, but that's not all. It's also lumpy and bumpy and humpy. If I turn my head slightly to the side, its lumpy-bumpy-humpiness becomes even more pronounced.

I jerk my head out of the angle and stare straight ahead at myself. That's better. When viewed straight-on, in strong daylight, my nose is passable. Like how Barbra Streisand's nose calms down when she's gazing directly at the camera. That's when you notice her cat-like eyes.

I practice rotating my head from side to side, then staring straight on. Alas, I have no "good side." Straight on is the only way. As of right now, this is the only angle from which other people will view my nose.

My plan goes into play the very next day. I don't socialize much at school, but whenever I do talk to the other kids, I hold my head absolutely still, staring straight at them, tilting my chin down to hide my nostrils. I can't tell if it's working, but it gives me something proactive to do.

Over time, I add movement to the pose. Using a mirror, I practice widening my eyes and expressing myself with my eyebrows. If I can keep people's attention up *here*, with their eyes locked on my cartoonishly active upper face, they won't look down and see my giant nose.

It is the perfect plan, and I have Barbra Streisand's album cover to thank for it.

When I talk to people, I treat them to intense eye contact and frequent eyebrow lifts. When the conversation is over, I whip myself around completely so they're left looking at the back of my head. I give nobody an angle view, and, even more importantly, no profile view.

Sometimes I use props. A pencil case covers a lot of nose, and so does my hand. If I reach up to adjust my bangs, I can keep my palm in the center of my face for a while. My bangs receive nonstop adjustments, especially when the lens of my dad's big 1980s camcorder is pointed my way.

Allow me to introduce Exhibit A: Several home movies featuring my hand in front of my face as I endlessly twiddle with my bangs.

The school year continues, and I get through more days with my hand in front of my face and only books for friends.

At least my teachers are nice to me. One of them, Mr. Houseman, takes the time to ask me, during one of my frequent fits of crying, what my problem is.

Oh, have I mentioned that I cry all the time? I do.

While my big ugly nose gushes snot, I sob to Mr. Houseman that I don't know why I cry all the time; I just do.

He kneels down and asks careful questions to ascertain if I'm being horrifically abused at home, like one of those kids in the gritty books I don't read. I understand where he's going with these questions.

I'm ugly, not stupid. I assure him nothing like that is happening. "I'm fine," I gurgle between sobs.

His eyes are as dry as mine are wet. They're brown and bulging and bloodshot. He smells like the teacher's lounge—coffee and cigarettes.

Rubbing his mustache, he asks, "Ruby, are you crying because you're nervous about the quiz this afternoon?"

The quiz? I don't even know which one he's referring to. Why would I care about a quiz? I ace every one of them.

"Maybe," I say tentatively, clinging to this possibility like a life preserver.

As I agree to his theory, the weight in my chest lightens. I *must be* upset about the quiz. I can't possibly be crying because I'm ugly and unlovable, and I'm still coming to grips with the idea that everyone dies—like, everyone!—and I am utterly alone in this world, stuck in a cold and unfeeling family, with not a single friend to call my own. It must be this afternoon's social studies quiz that's making me anxious. Good call, Mr. Houseman. I never imagined that I could take this bottomless sadness inside myself and blame it on something so simple. It's sublime, really.

My tears stop flowing. I wipe my nose with my sleeve, because kids don't carry handkerchiefs, even though they really should.

"You know, Ruby," Mr. Houseman says, rubbing his mustache in that teacherly way. "You'll be fine." He's still kneeling, so his long, serious face is at my level. Without blinking, he says, "Everything's going to be all right."

And that was it.

That day in the hallway outside the classroom, I didn't pour my heart out, and he didn't deliver an inspirational speech worthy of note in anyone's memoirs, except... he did. He took a moment to listen, and to offer hope to someone in pain. It didn't matter that he misunderstood the details. He cared enough to kneel down to my level and lie a little, uttering that magical phrase that can't possibly be true, but that we all long to hear spoken in a calm, reassuring voice.

Everything's going to be all right.

Mr. Houseman, and everyone else who teaches, or works with, or raises children with kindness and dignity, thank you.

* * *

Back to the present day, to me looking at myself in the mirror after the meeting.

It's no wonder people were avoiding eye contact. Staring at my reflection, I tsk-tsk myself for neglecting the lessons of my youth. Could I have looked more like human chopped liver if I'd tried? I wore no makeup, my hair was a disaster, and my clothes were the same shades of gray-brown as discount meat.

I was ugly. Next to the pretty blonde, I was Shrek. Not Princess Fiona, but Shrek.

And you know what? Rather than cry about my unattractiveness, I let out a laugh of relief.

I had been worrying all day that something was wrong with my personality. It turned out the problem was just my plain, dumb face! I can deal with that. I'll never win a beauty pageant, but I can apply enough dark eyeliner and lipstick to look decent enough in bright light, just like the aging actresses in *Ocean's Eight*.

Lesson learned! I need to wear flattering colors, fix my hair, and wear makeup to social events. Not unless I'm headed to a meeting for Ugly People Anonymous, UPA for short, where my issues will be overshadowed by people with inoperable goiters, birth defects, traumatic facial injuries, and other Real Problems.

By the way, I mention this fictitious meeting of the Ugly People Anonymous as a humorous way of letting you know that, yes, I understand that ugliness is not a disability. People who navigate the world from a wheelchair, or with a guide dog might love to trade problems with me.

But it's still important to acknowledge looks. Society's definition of beauty might be changing, but nothing's going to shift drastically in our lifetime. There is no denying nature. Scientific studies prove that some beauty standards are universal. Tiny infants, who don't read women's magazines, respond more favorably to people with balanced, symmetrical facial features. Our response to beauty is instinctive, not unlike our response to loud noises, sweet fruit, or big spiders.

What's more, a person's attractiveness, as rated by others, can be influenced by who's around them.

Let's say you're a knockout who usually rates an eight. If you hang out with your cousins, who are fives at best, you're going to average down to a seven in other people's eyes. This is a scientifically-proven fact that validates the existence of the Mean Girls Clique. It's to preserve their rating that the

Heathers demand a certain level of upkeep from their members.

How do you rate? I'm guessing it's not as high as you'd like.

Cheer up! There are benefits to being less than a perfect ten.

Do you know which women get to enjoy friendships with men who aren't just hanging around waiting for an opportunity to get in our pants? The average-looking ones.

And that's not all. We beauty-challenged females get to take breaks in between relationships. For as long as we like. We can read a book on the bus uninterrupted. We can enjoy dinner alone at a restaurant without having free cocktails sent to our table by an old guy who looks like our dad.

Get ready to put feeling bad about your looks on your fuck-it list. Here comes the rest of the sales pitch:

Do you have buckteeth and a weak chin? Get ready to save money during the summer wedding season. Nobody wants you as a bridesmaid, bringing down the group's average in the photos.

Are you not a supermodel? Come take a job working side by side with men. Men who won't be distracted by the crossing and uncrossing of our legs. Men who treat you with the same collegial disinterest they show beta males. You go, girl. You're practically equal to a beta male, except for the part where you get paid as much.

Even aging is easier for women who aren't losing the advantage of sexual desirability. Wallflowers don't suddenly become invisible at age forty, because we always were invisible.

And finally, everyone knows that homely girls have better personalities. And, my goodness, are we ever great in bed. We actually move around and everything. We may not be beautiful, but we can be all sorts of other adjectives, such as cute, or charming, or sultry, or surprisingly adept at kinky roleplay.

Fellas, if you're listening, take notes. If you want to be happy for the rest of your life, put a ring on that knock-kneed girl's finger. Your eyes might prefer the beauty queen, but a pretty girl who treats you like dirt won't look so pretty after a few years. Marry an ugly duckling, treat her right, and you'll have a sexy swan. Best of all, when you're photographed next to her, you won't look like Shrek.

NAPKINS

When I'm eating a meal at home, I never use a napkin.

But when I'm eating a meal at a restaurant, I always use a napkin.

What's that all about?

I have no idea. That's why this is the shortest chapter in the book.

BE GOODER
AT TALKING

I'm happy to report that the young heroine of our story thus far, little Ruby Rey, turned a corner at age twelve and a half, when finally she was adopted into a small social group.

I still remember the smile on Mr. Houseman's face when I asked if I could move my desk to be closer to some other girls. He looked so happy and relieved as he jumped into action, lifting my desk with one mighty arm and kicking furniture out of the way with his long legs.

And so, with those youthful lessons out of the way, we are jumping forward in time.

Welcome to Adulting 101 with Ruby Rey.

Should you be lucky enough to join a social group, you'll need to behave yourself so you don't get thrown out again.

Let's start with parties.

Children's parties are no problem, since there are adults around to supervise, and scary clowns to feast upon the bones of the naughty.

Grownup parties are more challenging.

When it comes to parties with adults, know that a good percentage of attendees don't even want to be there.

These people are called introverts. They only come because they agreed to when they were in a better mood, back when it was still daylight. Introverts spend their time at parties checking their phones and wondering what their pets are doing at home without them.

The other type of people who don't want to be at grownup parties are extroverts who suspect there's a better party going on elsewhere, perhaps one with fewer boring introverts.

Why do we have parties at all? It's silly to gather in dim rooms with loud music when we could be wearing stretchy pants and binge-watching crime dramas on Netflix while licking the potato chip salt off our fingers in the privacy of our own homes.

The reason is because deep down, on some primal level, we crave social contact. Solitary animals, such as badgers and sea turtles, don't feel the need to hang out with each other except for mating, but we humans are social animals. We want to be around the rest of the tribe.

Until such time as we evolve beyond this, why not make the most of it? Prepare to have fun with your fellow humans, and fun is what you shall have.

Let's say you've got your party invitation. Unless this shindig is a sexy partner-trading swap meet—in which case, go you!—the main thing you'll be doing there is making sweet love to identical twins. Oops. Wrong party. I meant to say you'll be making conversation with other people who don't want to be there.

PART I
RUBY REY'S GUIDE TO MAKING SWEET
CONVERSATION TO PEOPLE

There is one simple trick to good conversation. The trick is to not be bad at it.

There are two kinds of bad conversation makers.

The first group are Talky Talkers. These people believe that "talking to people" means, literally, talking to people. Talking and talking. Never listening.

Some Talky Talkers have learned to mimic good conversation, like how a parrot can mimic phrases. They will briefly close their talky holes and allow their partner a turn. All the while, however, the Talky Talker won't be listening. They'll be planning their next barrage of words, listening just closely enough to not miss their cue to begin yakking again.

Why do these people jibber jabber so much? I'm glad you asked. There are three reasons people talk too much.

Reason number one: Some people, including many extroverts, seize the opportunity to air their thoughts out loud because they don't talk to *themselves* enough.

These non-self-communicating folks aren't in touch with their emotions. They don't know how they feel about things until they hear the words coming out of their mouths. For these people, all talk is therapy.

Has one of them cornered you as their free therapist? Expect to see their face light up with multiple a-hah moments as they go on and on and on, making their discoveries.

All these people want to hear from you is a summary of what they're saying. Which can get a little dull because it's so one-sided. But hang in there. Nothing lasts forever.

If you happen to recognize yourself as this obnoxious person, the Out-Loud-Thinking Talky Talker, be assured you can change your ways. Try hiring a therapist, getting a life coach, starting a blog, writing in a journal, or putting on a disguise and facing the mirror.

If you chose the last option, try wearing a high-quality wig, then introducing yourself using a fake name and a sassy accent. Surprise! You're just talking to yourself in a mirror! Does this make you feel stupid? Well, of course it did. But now you'll find that, by comparison, writing in a journal or hiring a life coach seems a lot more reasonable.

Reason number two: Another explanation for compulsive talking—and probably the most obvious one—is that some Talky Talkers long to be noticed and admired.

Wanting to be noticed, admired, and thus given higher status is not crazy. Like craving social contact, it's a survival trait, dating back to a hairier time when we lived in caves. Back in the day, we used to pass around fire-roasted animal parts after the hunt, giving the choicest bits to those with higher status.

In modern times, excessive attention seeking in adults might be a compulsion that grew within, like a noxious weed, from a seed that was planted in early childhood, when their primary caregivers couldn't meet their needs. The squeaky wheel gets the grease, as they say.

If that's you, I'm sorry you weren't looked after better as a wee pup. The good news is you can use this attention-seeking, status-craving drive as a gift. Our most beloved entertainers and leaders come from this category. Boasty Talky Talkers, you can get the attention you desire, if you offer something of value in return. Know your audience and cater to their taste.

You can also counteract the downsides of your gift by becoming a better listener, which I'll get to shortly.

Reason number three: When people won't shut up, there's one less obvious yet common reason for it. These are the Anxious Talky Talkers. They keep busy babbling because they have an aversion to feeling strong emotions.

With these poor souls, their empathy is to blame. Contrary to popular belief, empathy can make for a terrible listener. For a sensitive, empathetic person, hearing someone else's problems leads to feeling and taking on those problems. Depending on who's doing the talking, this can be a scary proposition.

Even worse for these Anxious Talky Talkers is that dreaded and rare sound: Silence.

In the silence, they might have to feel *their own* emotions. So they turn on a video or a podcast, or they find a way to keep talking. The words have to keep flowing, just like that bus in the greatest runaway bus movie ever made, 1994's blockbuster hit, *Speed*. Anxious Talky Talkers are a lot like the GM New Look bus navigated by America's Sweetheart, Sandra Bullock. They can't slow down or they'll explode.

Can one overcome anxious talking? Yes. It's easy. Go to your friendly neighborhood sex toy shop and buy one of those ball gags.

Or, a more subtle method, for you chickens who aren't into ball gags, would be to work on recognizing the problem when it's happening, then engaging in helpful self-talk, and, finally, retraining yourself. Mindfulness or meditation can help with awareness and self soothing.

With patience and practice, you, too, can make an exciting transition. You can go from being a compulsive overtalker to being the miserable victim of someone else's compulsive overtalking. Enjoy your prize. You earned it.

In summary, people talk compulsively because they are trying to understand themselves, or they're insecure about their social status, or they're nervous about their emotions. It has everything to do with *their* issues, and nothing to do with the recipient. So don't take it personally when it happens to you. Try showing some understanding, respect, and compassion.

It's easy to make good conversation with people who are flawless. Pat yourself on the back if you can keep up on your end. Now, if you can bring the sparkle to interactions with people who aren't perfect, that is the real skill. For your efforts, you may win yourself a career connection, or a new friend for life.

Now that we've covered the issue of too much talking, we can deal with the other end of the spectrum: Boring McSnooze people who put you to sleep.

These folks seem pleasant enough at first, but after a few digs with your conversational shovel, there will be a metallic PANG. Bedrock. There's nothing beneath the pleasant topsoil.

Boring McSnooze people will never be cast on a reality TV show. On the plus side, they probably don't have the type of Cluster B personality disorder that would make them a viable reality TV show candidate. On the negative side, they're kinda dull. They never react emotionally or offer anything personal of themselves.

These yawn-inducing people don't just have boundaries. They have castle walls, and moats filled with alligators.

Why? The answer is right there in front of you. These people have strong, healthy defenses. If they're not letting down the drawbridge, that means you haven't yet earned your way into the castle.

Do you want in? If you do, you'll have to do a better job of winning the trust of His or Her Royal Highness. A good first step would be to stop sarcastically referring to them in your head as His or Her Royal Highness. Put them at ease; take your time.

Most humans aren't like sitcom pilots. They don't establish their hopes, dreams, and personality quirks in broad strokes to hook you in before the first commercial break.

If you recognize yourself as Princess Boring McSnooze, and you'd like to become more open, good for you. It can be done, and you don't need to memorize a list of current events.

The trick to being more open and interesting is to become a better listener. In fact, becoming a better listener might be the One Weird Trick that makes you better at everything in life. And I'm just handing it to you! Barely one third of the way into this book! My goodness. There's already been a lot of great stuff. And there's still so much more. But let's not get ahead of ourselves.

Get some Q-Tips, dig the wax out of your ear holes, and carry on to the next chapter.

BE GOODER
AT TALKING
PART 2

RUBY REY'S GUIDE TO LISTENING WITH ALL THE
EARS YOU'VE GOT

Nobody wants to be the sponge. Nobody signs up for a class about public speaking, or acting, or improv to get better at, ugh, *listening*. Isn't that just another word for letting the other person shine?

I'll admit that listening doesn't sound very sexy, but maybe you've never truly given it your all. You will be excited to give it another shot after I prep you with a few tips and tricks.

First, let's get the obvious part out of the way: Close your mouth. This will help your ears and eyes engage. Relax your jaw so you can hold this position without effort. You may wish to use this opportunity to run your tongue over your teeth for any stray food.

Next, listen to your conversation partner with a completely open mind. Easier said than done!

You've probably heard that phrase "open mind" before, but what does it mean? If you're like me, it's a loaded phrase. All my life, whenever people have asked me to have an open mind, it's right before they try to sell me something, like a starter kit in their pyramid scheme to sell makeup that's "not really makeup."

I bet when I used the phrase *open mind*, you clenched your jaw, tensed your body, and slammed shut your mind.

However, if your mind actually opened up on my command, come see me after this book. I have a wonderful opportunity for you to earn some money on the side...

Ahem.

Let's push aside the stale idea of having an "open mind" and use a new phrase: empty room. Let your mind be an empty room that could hold anyone or be used for anything.

When you're trying to be a better listener, think of the phrase *empty room*. Or whatever works for you. Blank sheet of paper. Huge concert hall. Wide open blue sky. I would suggest imagining the blank crust of a make-your-own pizza, but that might get you distracted, thinking about food.

Back to the empty room / blank sheet of paper / concert hall / blue sky.

The key is to let your mind be empty and spacious. Allow the other side of the conversation to flow into you and fill this empty space.

Then what? Nothing. You don't have to do anything consciously. Your mind is a riddle-solving supercomputer and loves taking in information. Let your amazing subconscious do its job.

There's only one thing you need to watch out for: Pre-planning what you're going to say next. When you're planning what to say next, you're no longer fully engaged in listening. If you do find yourself filling the empty room in your mind with your own plans, gently sweep those plans out the door.

You know how you've been meaning to meditate more or practice mindfulness? This is your chance, and you don't even have to squeeze into yoga pants or visit an ashram. Instead of a flickering candle flame or a ringing bell, stay empty and focus on taking in what your conversation partner is saying.

You will get a chance to contribute. Don't rush your entrance. Be quiet and let the punctuation marks be your guide. Do not speak until you've heard either a question mark or a period.

Your conversation partner will probably use a few commas while stringing ideas together. Don't start talking on a comma. No matter how long they go on talking, wait for the question mark or the period.

When you do hear the period, let out whatever breath you have inside your lungs. Don't speak yet. You can't anyway—not without air. Now breathe in.

A word of warning: There's a chance, that while you're breathing in and preparing to speak, your partner will bust in here with more talking. This is called being a Premature E-Talk-Ulator. This non-medical condition is rather unfortunate, but it does happen. The only way to stop a Premature E-Talk-Ulator is to grip their face between your palms and say, softly but firmly, "Nope."

Assuming your partner isn't a Premature E-Talk-Ulator, and they haven't cut you off by turning their period into a comma, you've now got your lungs full of good oxygen.

Here's the fun part.

Now, you will open your mouth, and—surprise, surprise—some totally fresh words that are relevant to the discussion will fall out of your mouth.

How can this happen when your head was so empty? It's magic! Or, as the scientific would say, it's your subconscious doing its job without your conscious awareness.

If you allow yourself to be truly spontaneous, not guarding your ego with preplanned responses, you'll surprise yourself. If you're surprised, your partner will be, too. And they'll love you for it. Who doesn't love a good twist? You'll both be hooked.

Repeat as necessary, being patient with your partner if they aren't perfect yet. Don't be too smug. You were lucky enough to read this book, and they haven't yet—not until you recommend it, hint hint.

How are things going?

If you're disappointed with yourself, remember to be patient. It takes a lot of effort to make any skill, conversation included, look effortless. Most of those "spontaneous" conversations you've seen on late night talk shows have been rehearsed. Plus both parties are professional entertainers.

It will be hard to retrain your old ways. You might believe you're listening when you're actually planning your next witty response. It's hard not to. Ideas will naturally bubble up while you're listening. So many ideas. The key is to let them go, like fish that are too small. Catch and release. That's how I think of my responses as they come swimming by before it's time.

Hello, little fish.

It's not time yet.

Goodbye, little fish.

Catch and release.

But what, you may be asking right now, *is the point of waiting for the next fish when the one swimming by right now looks perfectly adequate?*

Glad you asked!

There is a point to letting go of all responses that come before your partner's question mark or period.

Look at it this way: If you are a contestant on a TV quiz show, what happens if you buzz in prematurely, when the host is only a third of the way through the question?

You'll answer wrong, and you won't earn a lot of points. You might get negative points.

But conversations aren't TV quiz shows, you might be saying in a slightly whiny voice.

Oh, they aren't? Take away the cameras, and what have you got? Questions and answers.

That's why you wait for the right fish, the freshest one. That's the wittiest, most entertaining response. You'll look brilliant, and your conversational partner will be grateful.

Best of all, when you're living in the moment, your partner will relax and do the same.

This can be very handy if you're talking to an attractive person with whom you'd like to exchange more than words. Wow them with your listening skills, and it could lead to other things. They may want to touch the squirrel that lives in your pants!

RUBY REY'S BONUS TIPS
FOR MODERN SMALL TALK

Before we wrap up our segment on conversations, here are two important tips that aren't covered in any classic etiquette books.

Tip number one:
Never talk about binge-watching TV shows.

At 100% of all social gatherings that have happened in the post-Netflix era, no matter the size or location of said party, whenever the topic of a TV show comes up, an unfortunate pattern plays out.

First, there is a burst of excitement. Everyone's ears perk up. There's a group frenzy as people jump in, talking about one binge-worthy show, then another, and another. Gradually, excitement wanes.

Post-peak, there is a toothless disagreement about some series finale. Talk continues, but the mood never returns to its previous lofty heights. Shrugging begins. More shows are named. Postures slump and people drift away.

But one person won't let go of the topic. His name is Andrew, and he watches everything. It's not binge-watching; it's a lifestyle!

Andrew asks, "Have you seen this one yet? It's from Asia, where it's already huge!"

People respond to Andrew begrudgingly. "No, I haven't seen that one, but I've heard good things."

The conversation dies, circling the drain even as Andrew attempts CPR by excitedly listing off more obscure shows.

The party may continue for a while after this, possibly for hours, but everyone will know in their hearts that the party's true TOD, Time of Death, was much earlier. The party died when Andrew wouldn't stop badgering everyone to watch the dubbed English version of a Japanese-Taiwanese fantasy show about guardians of a sword because, even though the characters are puppets, and thus have a limited range of emotion, the writing is surprisingly nuanced and the visuals are a feast for the eyes.

"Sure, Andrew. We'll get right on it."

Tip number two:

Don't ever shut down a person for mentioning something they've already posted on social media.

If some poor soul shares with you a bit of personal news, and you reply with "Yeah, I know you just had a baby. I read that on your page," you might as well yawn directly in their face. Way to make a person feel like an unwanted recap!

Should you lose your manners and commit that conversational sin, do what you can to salvage the situation.

I have written for you a handy phrase that you can memorize and recite as needed.

Repeat after me: "While I did see that online already, I'm so glad we are face to face right now, because I definitely want to hear more about your new baby / gluten-free puff pastry / hand-made sweaters for orphan bats."

Then laugh self-consciously and continue:

"I can't believe I'm such a gaping asshole that I actually referenced social media as though it was a substitute for IRL conversation. What a relief it will be when the Singularity finally comes, and we're all digitally uploaded to the cloud while our mortal bodies are vaporized. Until that blessed day, I guess we're just living through this awkward transitional time, hauling around these fleshy meatbags."

Now punch them in the arm playfully.

STAB AWAY,
WITH CONFIDENCE

I'm in the car with my cousin, who's driving and talking to her female employee on speaker phone. My cousin runs a boutique flower shop, among other things. She's a busy lady who has multiple irons in the fire at all times. Like many busy ladies, she drives recklessly, yells at her family, and goes through a lot of chocolate and red wine.

At this moment in time, her female employee, whom I will call Zena, is trying to figure out the flower shop's accounting software.

Zena says, meekly, "I don't know what I'm doing with this accounting system. When can you sit down with me and show me how to use it?"

My cousin waves one hand over the steering wheel and says, "You don't need me there to hold your hand. What's the problem?"

"I don't know how to reconcile the bank account."

Another hand wave. "Oh, that's easy. You just check the totals and make sure everything matches, then you hit the reconcile button."

I can hear, over the speakers in the car, Zena's head being scratched. "What?" There's a sniffle. Naming her Zena for the purposes of this anecdote was a deliberately ironic choice, because clearly this Zena with a Z is nothing like Xena with an X, the Warrior Princess.

My cousin speaks slower and louder, losing patience. "It's easy. You can see the totals on the screen, right?" Her tone is patronizing.

"Uh... I see numbers."

"Now, Zena, you just have to make sure everything matches the paper statements. You don't need me there."

I hear the scuffling sound of Zena fashioning a suicide noose out of office supplies. She squeaks, "But what if they don't match?"

My cousin rolls her eyes and sighs. "You just have to correct the ones that don't match. Make the computer and the statements match."

There's a squeaking of chair wheels as Zena rolls back from her computer and scouts the ceiling for a sturdy beam to use for hanging her paper clip noose.

"You can do it," my cousin says, exasperated. "You just need to have confidence."

Their conversation continues for a while. I squirm uncomfortably in the passenger seat, and not just because my cousin isn't paying attention to the road we are speeding down.

There are many kinds of pains in the world, and one of them is the agony of having to be silent while someone gives out bad advice.

Fun tip: You can identify bad advice because it frequently has the phrase "you just" in front of some vague or meaningless instructions.

"You just have to be yourself."

"You just need to watch what you eat and exercise more."

And, worst of all, by a factor of one million, "You just need to have confidence."

This is not a chapter about how my cousin was wrong and I was right. I love my cousin, and not just because she was the best babysitter, who let me stay up late watching R-rated movies about teenaged hookers getting vengeance.

This chapter is about the perils of learning how to "just have confidence," how to "fake it 'til you make it."

Now, confidence is great. We all love confident people—usually because they have something to be confident about.

There are even times when faking confidence is the correct approach.

For example, let's say you're inside a cage full of hungry circus lions. You have no training with lions, but you have been armed with a whip and a chair. If those lions sense any weakness, they'll pounce. Now is the time to act confident. Act your ass off or get your ass bitten off.

However, when it comes to situations that don't involve hungry circus lions, bluffing—also known as fake-it-til-you-make-it style confidence—has very little value. And most situations that arise in modern life do not involve hungry circus lions.

What does have value, however, is the confidence of *actually being competent*.

The confidence of competence is harder to attain. It cannot be acquired at a workshop where you practice throwing your shoulders back in a power pose. The real path is a bit dull, really. One must put in the long hours to learn how to do the actual thing one wants to be confident in. Even lion tamers will tell you that learning how to actually train lions will do far better than fake confidence at reducing ass-bites.

When you know how to do something competently, you'll feel true confidence. It's only logical. When you've had success in the past at some activity, you have plenty of evidence that you'll be successful again, and that's where the confidence kicks in, naturally.

If some well-meaning person tells you to "just be confident," what they're really asking you to do is believe some fake history in which you've already successfully done the thing you're about to do. Sounds pretty crazy when I put it that way, right?

And yet people keep perpetuating this myth about confidence.

Whenever I encounter someone advising women to "apply a little more confidence," I scream inside my head: CONFIDENCE IS NOT LIPSTICK!

Confidence is not something you can screw out of a handy tube and apply as needed.

Speaking of lipstick, if people keep telling you that all you need is confidence, chances are good that you are female.

A woman seeking mentorship on her career path will be told, constantly and continuously, that the key to getting ahead is to have more confidence.

Meanwhile, a man who is seeking mentorship is far more likely than a woman to be taken under a wing by a male mentor, who will skip the confidence pep talks, and train his acolyte in, oh, *actual business tactics*.

What is this bullshittery?

It's the same old bullshittery. That's what it is.

The gender gap is as wide as it is stubborn, and no amount of rolling back one's feminine shoulders is going to fix it.

Studies have shown that women have just as much confidence as men, but they do not self-promote as much because there is a very real backlash that happens to women who toot their own horns. For women, finding the delicate balance between outward confidence and socially acceptable female modesty is almost impossible.

Worse, all the fear mongering about women not having enough confidence is perversely making the problem worse. Now women are internalizing this belief that we are somehow deficient, somehow lacking.

But if the problem of gender inequality can be blamed on this so-called "confidence gap," if the problem is simply that we girls can't get our panties unbunched long enough to rustle up some confidence, that means the ongoing problem of patriarchal oppression should be blamed on... us?

Yeah, I don't think so.

You, my skillful and powerful female friend, already have all the confidence you need. Don't waste one more minute feeling bad that you don't have more.

Your fight is not with yourself.

Your fight is with the system.

If you have a mentor who insists that all you need is more confidence, put that dummy on your fuck-it list and find a better mentor.

If you need skills, get those skills. Take a class, get a how-to book, watch videos online, volunteer as an intern. Build those skills. Get 'em! Beg, borrow, and stab your way to those skills.

On second thought, don't stab.

Unless you need skills in stabbing things, like you're trying to become the world's top shish kebab chef.

In that case, stab away.

WHO'S A
GOOD GIRL?

I walk in the door. I take off my shoes. I pick up my shoes. I put them in the closet.

Sometimes I narrate these actions in a song that sounds like a nursery rhyme: "I walk in the door. I take off my shoes. I pick up my shoes. I put them in the closet."

I have been doing this every single day for years, ever since I watched a video by Dr. BJ Fogg about developing habits. Not just any ol' habits. Dr. Fogg has trademarked the phrase Tiny Habits. He runs a program by that name, helping people change their lives one teensy weensy little bitty habit at a time.

Before I watched his Tiny Habits videos, the area near my front door was littered with between three and six hundred pairs of shoes. Whenever I expected company, I would shepherd those six to twelve hundred shoes into the closet so that visitors didn't trip on their way in and break a leg, or, worse, damage my favorite boots.

Whenever I tidied up, I admired the flow of the entryway. What excellent feng shui! But it didn't last long.

Then, one day, I stumbled across my first Tiny Habits video. *Interesting*, I thought. *This Fogg person is a real habits nerd. Maybe I'll give this a shot for a week before losing interest and forgetting it entirely.*

When it came to changing my habits, I was cynical. Over the years, I had bought plenty of things I never developed a habit for using: gym memberships, vitamins, linen pants, Rollerblades, extended warranties, a guitar, subscriptions to smart magazines I should be reading instead of watching TV in my sweatpants while licking potato chip salt off my fingers.

Despite my cynicism, I decided to try Fogg's Tiny Habits system to keep my entryway free of shoes.

The crux of the program is creating an anchor. An anchor is something you are already doing regularly, that can become the trigger for the new behavior. The anchor has to be specific and closely connected to the new habit.

When it came to putting away my shoes, walking in the door wasn't my anchor. Too vague. When stepping inside, I could already have groceries in my hands, or keys.

The correct anchor was taking off my shoes, which I always do. I don't wear shoes inside the house, unlike some people who enjoy bringing in the great outdoors and sidewalk loogies.

Once I'd identified the anchor, I had to forge a new connection in my brain, a new routine. You might think putting the shoes away was the new behavior.

But no! Surprise!

The new behavior should be much smaller, much *tinier* than that. The new behavior was picking up my shoes. That was it for step one.

True story: The day I started my new Tiny Habit, I practiced walking in the door, taking off my shoes, and picking up my shoes. I did this at least five times in a row to build muscle memory. After picking up my shoes, I would set them down, put them back on my feet, go outside, and do it all over again.

These are not the actions of a crazy person. These are the actions of someone who went on to develop a very solid habit.

Giggling at the ridiculousness of it all, I built onto the chain of habits. Picking up my shoes became the anchor for walking them over to the closet. Once I was standing in front of the closet with my shoes in hand, the rest came naturally.

This whole process struck me as hilarious. *I'm an adult. I'm relearning something children in preschool are trained to do.*

I took the shoes out of the closet, put them on once more, and went outside. I began vocalizing the steps in a fun, sing-song voice.

"I walk in the door. I take off my shoes. I pick up my shoes. I put them in the closet."

My husband, always happy to play games, was eager to join in the fun. He tried doing the same with his shoes, which had also been plaguing the front entryway.

As we performed the chain of habits together, we gave each other an embarrassed but giddy look.

"Yay for us," I said.

"We're doing it," He gave me a high five.

If you're already familiar with the Tiny Habits program, you'll note that we did our new routine perfectly. We made it simple, we made it fun, and once it was done, we allowed ourselves to feel wonderful.

Feeling good at the end of your new habit chain is just as important as having the anchor at the beginning. If something makes us feel good, we'll keep doing it.

Did you know you can make yourself feel good instantly? Without the use of red wine, or chocolate, or a vibrating cactus-shaped "back massager"?

It turns out we humans aren't that different from dogs. If you tell a dog it's a good boy or a good girl, their brains will light up with happiness.

"Who's a good girl? Missy is a good girl!" Picture Missy the Dog, wagging her tail and grinning deliriously. You don't even *know* Missy. She's just a dog tied up outside the grocery store that you stopped to say hello to. Her name probably isn't Missy, but she knows the words "good girl." All dogs do.

Humans have the same connection to the word "good." It is, I dare say, a sacred word.

People rarely use the word "good" in a sarcastic way. Sarcastic people say "That's just great," or "super," or "wonderful" when they mean the opposite.

Word nerds might point out that people might say "good" when something bad happens to a wrongdoer, righting the karmic balance. But even though those people are celebrating something negative, they're not being sarcastic. They feel this turn of events is good.

Good means good.

You can use this magical word on friendly dogs you encounter, and also with yourself.

There's no accomplishment too small to be celebrated with a private "good girl" to yourself. It's non-intoxicating, non-fattening, and doesn't drain your "cactus" batteries.

Remember the habit anchor, and remember the most important part: the celebration.

The second day of my new life as a person who has her shit so together that she even puts away her shoes, I experienced a spontaneous secondary Tiny Habit. Since I was standing in front of the closet anyway, I grabbed a hanger and hung up my jacket.

Boy, was that a surprise for the dining room chairs. Those chairs were used to wearing all my jackets whenever I wasn't.

Since that breakthrough, I've created numerous changes in my life using the program, but putting away my shoes is the one that will always be treasured.

That first habit was a keystone. It showed me what could be done, and Dr. Fogg also got me comfortable using positivity.

"Look at me, emptying the dishwasher while I wait for my coffee to brew," I might say to myself. "I could have pretended not to notice the other clean dishes when I grabbed my favorite coffee mug off the top rack, but I prevailed over laziness! Who's a good girl? I'm a good girl!"

I've lost track of the new habits I've trained into myself. That is the nature of habits; you think about

them a lot, and then, eventually, you don't think
about them at all.

HAPPINESS
ASSHOLES

I'm standing in the bustling heart of the farmer's market. The air smells of ripe fruit and fresh fish. Seagulls caw noisily as they steal french fries on the boardwalk, which is just outside the wide-open doors.

I'm here with my uncle, who's thinking about ordering gelato from one of the market vendors. He stares up at the chalkboard menu, his mouth open. He's an intelligent man, recently retired from the banking world, but in spite of his level of education, his mouth has a tendency to hang open. He's seventy-two, with neatly combed gray hair, sensible layers of clothing, and a pair of reading glasses tucked in his shirt pocket.

The crowd of tourists and locals bustle around us. The atmosphere is heavy with humidity and the din of multiple languages being shouted over the hum of coffee grinders and refrigeration units.

I'm not hungry, but I could eat. When I'm overstimulated by noises and smells like this, I always want to eat.

"My treat," I offer, hoping to speed the process along. "The gelato here is amazing."

My uncle accepts. After much deliberation, he selects the strawberry flavor. I pull out my wallet, but he insists on paying for his and mine. He is that kind of gentleman.

I watch him as he bites into the pretty pink gelato. His watery eyes light up like a little boy's. "It's ice cream," he says with wonder. "So, this is gelato. It tastes exactly like ice cream."

"Good, right?" I take a greedy chomp out of my own scoop of salted caramel.

He closes his eyes as he takes another taste. A pink dab sticks to the tip of his nose. He opens his eyes, smiling, and says, "The cancer loves the sugar."

The cancer loves the sugar.

He's referring to the malignant cells that have lately been winning the battle within his body. None of this is news to me. Cancer, and its treatment, are the reasons behind his visit.

It is late summer. He will be gone before the Halloween streamers and decorative gourds appear inside the farmer's market.

We stroll out through the doors to enjoy our gelato in the sunshine, both of us taking care to shield our food from the thieving seagulls.

As we meander down the boardwalk, the topic of his cancer is not revisited. I am relieved to keep talking about the sights and sounds around us.

He stops, finishing his strawberry gelato while he admires a wall of graffiti. I ask a passerby to take a photo of us. We pose next to a junk-art sculpture.

As I put my arm around him, my hand grazes the bony ridge of his protruding spine. He has lost more weight since his last visit. I have never truly understood the word *frail* until now. He is skin and bones.

Hours before this trip to the bustling, life-filled market, I sat next to him in a small hospital consultation room. Why are those rooms so inhumanely small? He spoke to the doctor about the tightness he'd been feeling in his shoulder blades. He wasn't complaining, just concerned.

The doctor leaned back and replied that some physical aches and pains were to be expected, given my uncle was—and this is a direct quote from the actual man's mouth, not a composite of heartless doctor clichés—"riddled with cancer."

Riddled.

Riddled is a bad word, used only to describe guilt, or mold, or bullet holes, or cancer. Nothing good can riddle.

My uncle and I pose between the graffiti and the junk-art sculpture, smiling for one last photo. I hug him to me as tightly as I can without hurting him.

* * *

Time passes. Decorative gourd season comes and goes. The grass grows over his grave.

I don't believe in an afterlife, yet I do indulge in a fantasy of my uncle being reunited "up there" with my aunt, a sunny woman who passed away a few years earlier, and whose favorite cardigan he kept draped over the passenger seat in his car.

When I think of my uncle now, I think of his legacy. It's about happiness. He often talking about happiness, and the secret to having it.

My uncle was not related to me by blood. That's how he escaped the family curse of being a miserable asshole. However, he didn't escape the curse of being another kind of asshole. He was kind of, well, it's hard to say. Let me be clear. I say this with nothing but love. He was a Happiness Asshole. He was an asshole *about happiness*.

I witnessed the intense judgment that came with his Happiness Asshole condition a number of times.

Whenever we encountered a grumpy person, he would comment on their attitude. He would wonder aloud why that person didn't choose, like he did, to be happy? He always chose to be happy, and he was dying. Dying! Why couldn't other people, who probably weren't even dying, also choose happiness?

After every visit to the cancer clinic, he would speak, with distaste wrinkling his thin nose, about how disappointed he was by the other patients. Oh, how they moaned and complained. Oh, how exhausting it was to be around their defeatist attitudes.

"They'll be dead within months," he'd say ruefully, shaking his head. Some people *did not* have a good attitude about their cancer!

My sweet uncle, bless his heart, believed it was his sunny disposition keeping him alive.

Maybe it did help. He was optimistic enough to comply with his treatments, and surely that extended his life.

But the main reason he had survived so long was because his cancer was the slow-moving type, a tortoise of a malady—not one of those freight train monsters.

I respected my uncle too much to disagree about his views on happiness. To his face, anyway.

You've probably had some Happiness Assholes in your life.

They mean well, but their understanding of other people doesn't go very deep. They judge everyone by their own set of values, and it doesn't stop at happiness. They also judge others for being in any predicament they wouldn't be likely to find themselves in. Happiness Assholes ask a lot of rhetorical questions, such as:

Why doesn't everyone drive the same speed I do?

Why don't the poor get better jobs and pull themselves up?

Why doesn't that young man get a pair of pants that don't fall down?

Why hasn't that mother taught her filthy children not to lick all the serving spoons at the salad bar? I was looking forward to eating a spinach salad with ricotta cheese, not contracting a new strain of viral hepatitis.

Happiness Assholes can't understand why everyone in the world hasn't chosen to be exactly like them. Never mind that they got their first cushy job through a family contact and never worked a single shift at a fast food joint. "That wasn't much of an advantage," they'll insist if you bring up their privilege. With hard work, anyone could have gotten to where they are. Why, if circumstances had been different, and they had been the one starting out as a fry cook, they would have knuckled down and worked their way up to CEO with a smile on their face!

Sure.

Sure, they would have.

That's what they have to keep telling themselves.

Being judgmental is a great way of getting out of feeling guilty. If a person believes that everything they have—money, power, respect—is freely available, and could be acquired by anyone at any time, they don't have to feel bad about having what other people do not. They don't have to acknowledge their own privilege. They deserve everything they have, just like how that mother with the unruly children deserves the new strain of viral hepatitis currently being dribbled onto her.

The Happiness Asshole might even say, huffily, "Those kids of hers look like they come from different fathers. Honestly. Some people and the choices they make."

Well, I've got a big headline for all the Happiness Assholes of the world, and here it is.

YOU DIDN'T CHOOSE TO BE HAPPY, YOU BIG DUMMY, SO STOP BEING SO SMUG ABOUT IT.

People can't simply *choose* to be happy because nobody can choose what emotion they feel.

Emotions don't work that way.

You can choose to be happy no more than you can choose to be sad, choose to be six feet tall, or choose to be a lottery winner with twelve million fuck-off bucks.

Yes, people can choose to make certain choices that may lead to different emotions. We can also reframe events to gain a different perspective. We can even partake in CBT—which stands for Cock and Ball Torture, and also for Cognitive Behavioral Therapy. Either of those CBTs could lead you down a different path with different emotions, but you can't simply choose to feel one emotion over another.

I know how emotions work for one simple reason: I am a professional writer.

Because I'm a professional writer, I understand something called an MRU. That acronym is not a sex thing—that I know of. It's the foundation of all stories. If a story is a brick wall, then the MRU is the individual brick.

Intrigued yet?

If you're still curious about this MRU thing, even though it's not about kinky sex stuff, step right this way.

Writers are not bound by the same rules as magicians and illusionists. I'm allowed to reveal the tricks of my trade.

In our next exciting chapter, you'll enter that sacred space: the Writer's Room.

THE DO-SOMETHING
DOORS

Thanks for joining me here, in the Writers' Room.

See that big corkboard over there, with the multi-colored index cards? That corkboard is where the magic of story plotting happens.

It's no coincidence that every police procedural show includes the following elements:

- a sympathetic victim
- an absurdly high-tech holographic crime scene reenactment
- a big plot twist right before every commercial break

Those elements are strategically placed, by the show's writers, to hold your attention. When a story is planned and executed well, it's a powerful thing.

But, despite all the multi-colored index cards on all the corkboards in Hollywood, some shows are still duds. You've likely found that even some episodes of your favorite shows are duds.

So, when good shows go bad, what went wrong?

If you're not a writer, you won't be able to pinpoint the exact problem with a show. Is it the acting? Cheap special effects? The fact that your potato chip bowl is empty?

Eventually, you'll grumble, "This is just *too stupid*," and you'll quit the episode. You are right to do so. Once a show reaches a critical level of stupidity, continuing to watch will bring you no pleasure.

If your spouse, or roommate, or the sentient lump that shares your sofa insists on finishing the stupid show, you have my sympathy. I sure hope your spouse, or roommate, or sentient lump has other good qualities to make up for their lack of instinctive understanding of human behavior.

I'm a professional writer, so it's easy for me to pinpoint the problems in this week's episode of *Tough Cops Learning How to Love Again*.

The problem is rarely the overly complicated crime, or the convenient string of tantalizing clues. We all love that stuff. It's what we signed up for— the stranger, the better. A dead hobo in an alley isn't intriguing. A dead hobo who mysteriously appears on a Russian space station orbiting Earth, now that's something to watch. We want to be puzzled, so a far-fetched premise never turns us off.

What does turn us off is that moment where the private detective, or tough cop, or space vampire does something... not stupid, exactly, but *unmotivated*.

Unmotivated is when the private detective / tough cop / space vampire goes into the spooky house / crack den / haunted space station without waiting for the backup that will be arriving in two minutes because, well, just because.

You might yell at the screen. "Don't go in there!" You turn to the sentient lump that shares your sofa and ask, Why is he going in there? Why not wait for backup? They're coming in two minutes!

There is a reason the detective runs in without waiting for backup.

Stop yelling and look at the screen now, a moment later. It's a commercial, right?

See, the writers needed to get the detective into some hot soup so you'll get agitated. That's how they keep you glued to the channel. Now you're watching the commercials. This show has been brought to you by various pizza delivery services, as well as by XERQUIZED, the new medication that combats the terrible health effects of the TV-watching and pizza-delivery lifestyle.

Now you get it.

The writers of *Detective Badass Punches Everyone* need to keep your eyes on the screen, and they hope you're too lazy to notice *their* laziness. You might ask, *Why don't the writers do their job and write a show that always makes sense and doesn't have plot holes?* Good question. Let me ask you something. At your job, do you get enough time, support, and hours in the day to do every one of your duties perfectly every time? Mm hmm. That's what I thought.

Now, nobody gets into writing so they can write shoddily. We pen monkeys are trying to do the best we can with finite resources. But sometimes the MRUs get shoved aside so we can stress you out before the commercial break.

What's an MRU, you ask?

MRUs OR MOTIVATION REACTION UNITS

M: The first letter of the acronym stands for Motivation.

Motivation for a character can be big or small. It can be a runaway dump truck heading straight for them, or a gust of wind that gives them goosebumps. It can be an army of the undead rising from their graves, or a dripping water faucet that goes PLIP PLOP all night. Motivation is anything that nudges a character into taking action.

In any movie, TV episode, or novel, there's one key Motivation, near the beginning of the story. It's called the Inciting Incident. This stimulus starts a chain reaction of MRUs. Every Motivation event kicks the main character into action, and also hooks you, the audience.

R: The second letter of MRU stands for Reaction.

Reaction is where things get tricky, because within that letter R, there are three components of character reaction. They are:

1. Emotion
2. Reflex
3. Rational action or speech

The first part, Emotion, is visceral and happens fast. It's a feeling. I'm assuming you know all about feelings. Here's a refresher: Some sample feelings are amusement, anger, annoyance, anguish, and anxiety—and those are just the A-word feelings.

There are many feelings with names, and even more that don't have names, at least not in English.

In German, there's *schadenfreude*. Schadenfreude is a type of pleasure one gets from another person's misfortune.

In Danish, there's *hygge*. Hygge is the deep sense of place, warmth, friendship, and contentment.

Emotions are instinctive, part of our survival system. They helped humanity reproduce and stay alive. It's easy to see how, when you look at the emotion of fear. Fear is what keeps small children from being eaten by clowns.

The part that comes after Emotion is Reflex. This one also happens fast. We have little to no control over our reflexes. For example: If something near us is falling, we'll reach for the falling object without thinking.

What makes something a reflex is the fact we do it without conscious thought.

Many reflexes bypass our brain entirely. When our bodies do something without getting orders from the brain, it's called a *reflex arc*. It's a reflex arc that makes you yank your hand away when you touch something hot. Another reflex arc causes the muscles in your eyes to adjust your irises in response to light. Yet another reflex arc causes your hand to shoot forward and grasp the cupcakes with the pretty pink frosting, and then mash them into your mouth. That's why bakeries have to keep the cupcakes behind glass!

Thanks to our reflexes, we do "smart" things, like jumping out of the way to avoid being hit by a dump truck.

Unfortunately, our reflexes also make us do things we'd call "stupid," such as reaching for a falling knife that might slice our hand.

Reflexes are neither smart nor stupid. They're simply reflexes.

When it comes to catching dropped knives, you can retrain this reflex. But you need to intentionally practice letting the knife fall. This skill is taught at chef training schools. Great teachers know that people can modify their reflexes, but it does take training that's deep, and consistent, and repeated. We call this *muscle memory*.

If you haven't retrained your reflexes, you still have your Factory Default Settings. Don't beat yourself up for the settings that came preloaded.

After emotion and reflex, the third and final part of Reaction is—at last!—Rational Action or Speech. This is where conscious thought kicks in. Finally.

On top of your emotions and reflexes, there's another layer of awareness. This awareness is like a teacher returning to the classroom after a ten minute break, and encountering pure chaos. This awareness says, "What the hell is going on in here?"

When the teacher is back in the classroom, it's time for your brain to do its job. And by "your brain," I specifically mean your frontal lobe. Your brain never takes a break, which is why you keep breathing and digesting at all times.

Your frontal lobe is located at the front of your brain, hence the snazzy name.

The frontal lobe provides your consciousness, judgment, and ability to curse at bad drivers in the language of your choice. The frontal lobe makes up 38% of your cerebral hemispheres. As for the rest of your brain, 7% of your gray matter is in charge of sweating from your armpits during scary movies, and the other 55% is, as we all know, your untapped psychic powers.

Once your frontal lobes kick in, you're operating on more than pure instinct. But this executive control is gradual.

If something exciting has happened, you'll have plenty of fresh chemicals in your system. Your adrenal glands, located at the top of each kidney, squirt adrenaline as needed. These glands produce other hormones, too. There's aldosterone, cortisol, noradrenaline, adrenal androgens, and more.

As the teacher regains control over the classroom, your frontal lobes help you become aware of the wider picture of what's happening. Now you are able to choose your actions. You can override the messages your hormones are sending your body and use your free will—assuming you believe in free will. Whatever course of action you take next, you are legally liable for what you do.

If you smash your fist through the bakery display case and grab the pretty pink cupcakes, you will have to pay for the damages.

* * *

A quick recap of MRUs:

M is for Motivation, which is anything that happens to a person and affects them.

R is for Reaction, which has three parts: Emotion, then Reflex, then Rational Action or Speech.

All that's left is U, which stands for Unit. Easy enough. And now we're done.

We have covered Motivation Reaction Units, or MRUs. MRUs are the basic building blocks of human behavior. Here they are in action:

Miss Muffet is eating breakfast when a Motivation event happens: A spider drops down beside her.

Miss Muffet's Reaction comes in three parts.

First comes Emotion. She's frightened.

Then, Reflex. She leans away from the scary spider instinctively. Her arms stiffen and pull up to shield her face. Her breakfast bowl goes flying. A shriek comes out of her mouth. She didn't plan to do any of these things; they just happened by reflex.

Finally, a few seconds later, there's been enough time for conscious thought to kick in. Her frontal lobes piece together what's happening. Physically, Miss Muffet's tunnel vision relaxes as the adrenaline wears off. Now she leans over and examines the spider, which turns out to be plastic, and attached to a string.

When she realizes the spider is fake, that becomes a new Motivation event. She feels outrage about having been tricked. Her fists clench by reflex to her anger. She follows the spider's string to her bratty older brother, who appears to be delighted. Miss Muffet howls angrily and then pushes him over, because she is only four years old and hasn't yet mastered control over her emotional impulses. If Miss Muffet were, say, twenty-four years old, she could be charged with assault for choosing to push over her brother.

The Miss Muffet scenario contains at least two MRUs, with two big emotions. Fear, and then outrage.

Next comes yet another MRU. Big Brother Muffet experiences a Motivation event when his sister pushes him over. He yells for their parents and claims that his little sister pushed him over for no reason at all. Brothers! And so life continues, one MRU after another.

* * *

Now, back to that badly written episode of *Tough Cops Learning How to Love Again.*

Bad writing happens when writers ignore basic human psychology and force their characters to take illogical actions in order to make certain plot points happen.

We humans are instinctively repulsed by behavior that is illogical. It's another survival trait that helps us avoid liars and their traps.

We do not pay attention to liars, or at least we don't for very long. Our tolerance for lies is about seven minutes.

Why seven minutes?

Ah. Let's get away from hour-long police procedurals and move over to that other TV staple, sitcoms.

Sitcoms regularly disobey the MRU rules of normal human behavior. The characters in sitcoms have their own rules, because the writers of sitcoms need to deliver comedy at a rate of five to seven jokes per minute. Normal human beings never communicate at a rate of seven jokes per minute.

We know that the characters in sitcoms are behaving falsely, but we allow it because we enjoy the jokes. We enjoy it for all of half an hour, or twenty-two minutes minus ads. At an average joke rate of 7 jokes per minute, that works out to 154 jokes per episode.

You may be scratching your head. There are over a hundred jokes in a sitcom? That can't be right. You've never laughed one hundred laughs at a single episode of anything, not even after eating special brownies.

Of course you haven't. But a joke doesn't need to get a laugh to be labeled a joke. To qualify, it needs to have two parts: setup plus punchline. Some of these jokes land, some don't. Didn't like that joke? No worries. Another one will be along in ten seconds.

Pop quiz time!

Name a one-hour sitcom.

Any one-hour sitcom.

You can't, can you?

If my question brought anything to mind, it's not a true sitcom. The show you're thinking of is probably a comedic drama or a sketch show.

For you sticklers, yes, there are a few one-hour sitcoms in existence, but they're obscure and the rare exception to the rule.

The reason we don't have one-hour sitcoms isn't because we'd get tired of laughing. We'll happily watch two or three different sitcoms back to back. The reason is we cannot tolerate more than twenty-two minutes of an unrealistic plot line.

Hell, we don't even like twenty-two minutes of it. Most sitcoms have three separate plot lines running through the episode. Broken down, each of the individual subplots takes only seven minutes.

Therefore, the maximum human tolerance for bullshit is about seven minutes.

* * *

Now you understand how sitcoms work and why bad writing is bad.

But, you may be wondering, what does any of this have to do with my happiness?

It's best explained by an example:

Miss Muffet is eating breakfast when a Motivation event happens: A huge, terrifying spider drops down beside her.

Miss Muffet simply smiles and continues eating her breakfast, because Miss Muffet has decided to be happy at all times, no matter what.

The spider, which is both very real, and a badass poisonous bastard, bites her leg. Miss Muffet continues to be happy and eat her cereal because she has decided to be happy at all times, and see the good in everything, no matter what.

Not a very good story, is it? It doesn't work. Not unless Miss Muffet is an elderly monk who has spent years meditating to change her instinctive reflexes to every type of motivating stimulus.

Most of us aren't monks, so when you hear someone declare that "happiness is a choice," don't feel bad that you don't share their delusion.

Don't beat yourself up over your inability to walk through the Choose Happiness Door.

The Choose Happiness Door doesn't exist!

According to the laws of MRUs, if you want to be happy, you'll need to have positive Motivations.

There are choices you can make to assist the universe in delivering positive Motivations to you.

As we learned in the chapter about Tiny Habits, you can deliver nuggets of happiness to yourself when you give yourself a few words of encouragement for accomplishments, big or small.

Also, you can choose to spend time with a person or pet who makes you happy. Or you can look around to see if someone else could use a hand or a friend. Or you can finish that thing you've been meaning to finish.

If you want to be happier, you gotta do something. Not everything you try is going to work out, but you have to keep trying things to find what works for you. If you do nothing, nothing's going to change. Few positive Motivations will come your way on their own.

But what about praying? Praying works for many people, even—surprisingly enough—atheists. Either it's the invisible hand of a divine entity or source energy that assists even the nonbelievers who ask for help, or it's because praying does count as doing something. In praying, you are calming your physical body while priming your brain to be open for solutions to problems. Sounds a lot like manually activating that teacher in the classroom, the executive function of the frontal lobes.

THE DO-SOMETHING DOORS

The big three Do-Somethings for happiness are:

- learning new skills
- completing tasks
- helping others

There is no Happiness Door. Only the Do-Something Doors, which may eventually lead to happiness.

You may note that none of these categories of actions are modern inventions. These rules run deep within us. Our cave dwelling ancestors survived because all of these actions helped individuals as well as the group to reproduce and survive. We are primed to work together, to be positively rewarded when we take actions that benefit the tribe.

Our tribe is much bigger these days, which is a modern invention. We're all grappling with that because it's relatively new. The internet is very new. Even the printed word is relatively new. We face so many challenges that are brand new.

But we'll figure it out. We always do.

* * *

In summary, this MRU concept is a bit advanced, so don't feel bad if you got a bit lost. There are plenty of highly-paid writers who don't even understand it.

I wasn't sure about including it in this book, but it has helped me so much in my own life that I figured *what the hell.*

If you take away only one key fact, let it be that all our emotions are responses. We can't choose our emotions directly, only indirectly by taking actions that may result in positive things happening to us.

If things were different, and we humans could feel any emotion we want, on command, with no side effects, humanity would go extinct within two generations. Let's hope science never gets us there.

The next time someone suggests that you "choose to be happy," pull out your fuck-it list and write the following: There is no Choose Happiness Door. There are only multiple Do-Something Doors.

PRAISE

My husband walks into the kitchen. He exclaims, "Wow! Someone really cleaned up in here."

"It was me," I squeal excitedly from my seat at the table.

"Good job, baby." He walks over to reward me with a kiss. "It looks really good."

"I know," I agree, nodding. "I slayed it."

"You sure did." He gives me a high-five before getting a glass of water.

We carry on with our day.

This sort of interaction is not an unusual occurrence in our household. My amazing husband, who is not being held captive against his will, regularly heaps praise on me for doing everyday things. He always did, but it took me a while to get used to it.

The first time he congratulated me for cleaning the kitchen, the interaction did not go so well.

Let's travel back in time, back to fifteen years ago.

The kitchen has been recently cleaned up, by me. My then-boyfriend enters the kitchen, looks around, and says, "Wow! Someone really cleaned up in here."

I look up from the magazine I'm reading, frown, and reply, "What the fuck is that supposed to mean?"

He, dumbfounded, says, "Uh... The kitchen was a disaster. And it looks nice now. I guess you cleaned it?" He tilts his head and gives me a puppy dog look.

I snort. "Don't patronize me."

"Uh..." He blinks rapidly. He has forgotten what he came into the kitchen for, but it certainly wasn't for a fight. He ducks his head and quickly leaves.

I stay where I am, scowling after him as he disappears.

What was that all about? Is he trying to manipulate me? Train me? If he thinks it's my job to clean the kitchen just because I'm the woman, he's in for a surprise. That's the last time I clean the kitchen. The *last time*.

Eventually, despite my threat to never clean again, I do. I am not the best housekeeper, but I will run the dishwasher when I'm completely out of clean plates and other flat things I can eat off.

Again, my man compliments me on the job well done.

Again, I react with suspicion.

Again, he reacts to my suspicion with confusion.

What he doesn't know, because it's still early in the relationship and we haven't yet delved that deeply into my emotional baggage, is that I am deeply suspicious of praise.

I'm suspicious of praise for the same reason I'm leery of eating things with tentacles. Some people grew up eating tentacles, so it's no big deal for them.

I did not grow up eating tentacles. I also did not grow up receiving praise.

When I was a kid, any time I did a household chore without being screamed at to do so, my efforts were met with derision:

"You put away your laundry already? You must want something."

"You vacuumed without being asked? You're hiding something. You must be pregnant."

And, my absolute favorite, "You're up early this morning. Did you wet the bed?"

Now, I know that these backhanded compliments would not make the list of top terrible crimes perpetuated on children by their parents, but this type of emotional manipulation does have a lingering effect. These mind games are a subtle form of gaslighting. The parent pushes the child into having a bad reaction so that the "adult" can then mock the child for their childish reaction. "Oh, honey, you're overreacting again. It was just a joke. Don't be so sensitive."

Perhaps this hazing can play a positive role in raising humans. It might teach children how to get control over displaying their emotions.

However, there should be balance. Children need to have their positive behaviors recognized, not turned into negative experiences.

Growing up, being raised by assholes, I didn't have my good qualities pointed out very much. It doesn't take a team of top psychologists to connect the little girl who never did anything praiseworthy to the adult woman who reacts to praise with angry suspicion.

Now, I *say* it shouldn't take a team of top psychologists to connect the dots, but, in my case, it did take at least one.

I never meant to get therapy. I thought therapy was something only people in Woody Allen movies did.

I wound up in a therapist's office because I promised my family doctor I would go for at least one session. That was the bargain I struck in exchange for a prescription for antidepressants. I believed that any therapist would confirm that my depression was purely chemical, and all I needed was pills. I randomly picked a clinic from the phone book and went in for what I knew—I knew!—would be my first and last appointment for silly talk therapy.

On an overcast Tuesday afternoon, I entered the clinic. It was eerily quiet. The waiting room was decorated with rocks engraved with words like *breathe* and *relax*.

My therapist was a white-haired, soft-spoken woman in a long dress. She led me into a small room with yellow walls, where I took my seat in a threadbare recliner. She barely had a chance to introduce herself before I began bawling my friggin' eyes out. I'd already been taking medication for a few weeks by this point, but it did nothing to hold back the tide of tears.

Bless her heart, the woman handled my breakdown like the professional she was. The session ended with me booking my next appointment.

In the year that followed, I learned a lot about myself, and I learned a lot about therapy.

Here's what surprised me the most: My therapist reacted to the things I said in the exact opposite way that everyone who was not my therapist reacted. Talk about getting a whole new perspective on, well, everything.

It is thanks to the hard work that began that day in therapy that I am now able to not just accept praise from my spouse, but revel in it. Also, now that my husband understands all the many things I struggle with, he has expanded the range of achievements he praises.

I have been complimented on a number of lofty achievements, including but not limited to the following:

- practicing basic hygiene by showering at least once every two days
- keeping my mouth shut while an elderly family member trash-talks a family member not present
- getting out of bed before noon

And today, during the writing of this chapter, I was given a big hug for taking the cat litter out to the garbage can, a task I usually avoid, claiming the bag is "too heavy."

My husband noticed the task had been done and said, "You took out the cat litter? All the way to the garbage can? Good job! You get a hug."

I melted into his embrace.

Forget bundles of red roses or fancy nights on the town. This expression of love is all I need.

BADLANDS OF
UNHAPPINESS

Dr. Ben-Shahar, the author of *Happier*, talks a lot about four quadrants.

He suggests sorting people into those four quadrants, the way the Sorting Hat in the Harry Potter series puts young wizards into Hufflepuff, or Gryffindor, or Pumpkin Spice Latte, or whatever the other Hogwarts houses are called.

Isn't his idea of finding your spot within a quadrant clever? Deep down, we all want to be sorted and categorized. The appeal of taking one of those online quizzes is finding out what flavor of screw-up you are. We humans are powerless before the temptation to get sorted, labeled, and prescribed treatment.

I know Zodiac signs are bullshit, and yet, if I'm waiting for my coffee and discover the day's horoscopes have been cut from the newspaper and taped to the counter, you'd better believe I'll be reading mine.

I could lie to myself and believe I'm only reading my horoscope to pass the time, the way one might take an interest in the ingredients of a shampoo bottle while on the toilet. But that doesn't explain why I'm only reading the horoscope that is specifically for my Zodiac sign.

Unlike horoscopes, Dr. Ben-Shahar's four quadrants are actually useful to intelligent people such as you or I. There's a reason the dude teaches courses on happiness at Harvard. His work is fantastic, and I highly recommend reading *Happier*.

Personally, I put my own little twist on Ben-Shahar's work.

I don't think of his happiness types as four quadrants, but as—hold onto your Sorting Hat—three circles. These three circles overlap, and the center, which would be three layers deep if you made the circles out of cake, is the sweet, triple-layer spot of happiness. If you're a smarty pants, you'll know these overlapping circles have a name. It's called a Venn diagram.

Fun fact: Venn diagrams were invented in 1880 by a guy called John Venn, who was too modest to name them after himself. He referred to his invention as Eulerian Circles. Not as catchy.

Now that you're picturing three overlapping circles, be they made of cake or other materials, imagine that the outer part of the circles, the single layers, are the badlands. Nothing but stinky swamps, sucky quicksand, and crying in the shower.

People wind up marooned out there in the badlands because, ironically, they were successful at finding a solid coping mechanism. Where they went wrong was in using that one coping mechanism for everything. When you lean too heavily on a single strategy, you risk becoming unbalanced. The badlands are called Nihilism, Hedonism, and Workaholism.

NIHILISM

What a scary word! It conjures up no positive connotations.

Who would willingly choose Nihilism as a life philosophy?

You know how they say the road to Hell is paved with good intentions? People who wind up in the Nihilism badlands might have started their journey to happiness with the best intentions. Maybe they took a meditation workshop and found it freeing. *Let go*, the meditation people say. *Let it go*, sings every kid after watching Disney's *Frozen* for the millionth time.

If anyone knows how to truly *let it go*, and live with the wind of their own rage inside their ice castle of solitude, it's Nihilists.

These are people who take perfectly good advice about letting go of attachments, then take it way too far. You can spot these people raving about letting-go books such as *The Life-Changing Magic of Tidying Up* by Marie Kondo.

A Nihilist, assuming they're not glued to the couch with depression, will spring into action after finishing a book about letting go of clutter. They'll gleefully toss out everything they have, since none of it sparks joy. What is joy, anyway? Life is meaningless and nothing works out or matters in the end.

Nihilists would love to live in an ice castle, as long as it's not too homey. Just a pure, crystalline structure with no sentimental clutter, please.

Keepsakes and tchotchkes are for the tasteless and weak.

When it comes to achieving ultimate minimalism, these folks push up their sleeves and get to work. They throw out half-burned candles, untouched birthday gifts, and ratty t-shirts. Then, when that's not enough to give them the echoing emptiness they crave, they move on to discarding perfectly good t-shirts, and brand new t-shirts they just got last month. And then, since they've got the garbage bags lined up anyway, why not toss out all their hopes and dreams? Ah, it feels so good to let go of those things.

Let it go, let it go, let it all go.

If you don't have hopes and dreams, you can't be disappointed when they don't come true.

When I was younger, I imagined Nihilists as skinny, artsy people who lived in the sixties, wore black turtlenecks, read Nietzsche, and smoked clove cigarettes. But there are plenty of Nihilists around to this day. You know a few.

- There's the hilarious mailman who, when greeted with a "good morning," tosses back his signature catchphrase, "What's good about it?"
- Or the gossipy girlfriend who always has the juicy details about someone else's life falling apart.
- The wedding guest who comments that "it won't last."
- Or the grumpy teenager. Teenagers are exceptionally good at Nihilism.

Nihilists aren't entirely bad to be around. They can be witty, with their cutting insights and their acidic sarcasm. They put the dark in dark humor.

Nihilists are reassuring, because they remind us, constantly, that things could always be worse. There's comfort in their predictability, which is why every great sitcom has one.

Also to their credit, Nihilists are great at making bold choices, since they believe nothing matters in the end.

But the problem with Nihilists is they will suck the life out of everyone around them.

Have you talked face-to-face with a Nihilist? It's like being held in a tractor beam. While they're sharing their cutting insights, they're watching your reaction closely. Not because they find you attractive. They're waiting for that magical moment when the glint of life dies out of your eyes.

They're serial killers of joy.

They can't help themselves. They can see the future, and they know—they just know!—that things always end badly. When they crush your big plans, it's only because they mean well. They're helpers at heart. Don't you want to avoid the inevitable disappointment that befalls all suckers who are naive enough to believe in something?

Nihilists take pride in having all the answers. They're smarter than everyone else. Won't you please acknowledge how clever they are? Now that we've established they know better than you, it's time to open up and feed these emotional vampires all your joy! Now is your chance to let it all go. They're the black plastic garbage bags for whatever you might be holding onto, you clingy weirdo.

Oh, no! You've fallen prey to a Nihilist? What do you do now? If you're not willing to release all hope and joy, fake it. Be like those mama birds who pretend to have a broken wing in order to lead a predator away from the nest. Positivity is not your friend when you're dealing with these darklings. Don't smile. You'll never win them over with your sunshine; it will only make them double down. Make your face solemn as you search out the nearest exit.

You can't win with these people. They'd rather be right about everything sucking than be proven wrong and wind up, ick, *having a nice time*. Nice times are for losers.

If you have any Nihilists in your life, encourage them to keep working on their brilliant webcomic or scathing standup routine, and leave you alone.

HEDONISM

These are the badlands that don't look that bad from the outside.

When I say Hedonist, do you picture someone in a toga, reclining on a sofa, demanding their servant feed them more peeled grapes?

Good. That's a fine example of a Hedonist.

In regular, non-cartoon life, the Hedonist is your lazy coworker who constantly talks about their last vacation or their next one.

The Hedonist is totally going to get their life together, but first they need a good massage and a week at the spa so they can get their head on straight, you know?

Hedonists aren't all bad. When your birthday comes around, they give the best gifts. They tell you about the newest, trendiest restaurants. If you need a shopping buddy, your Hedonist friend will drop whatever they're halfheartedly working on and jump at the chance to hit the mall. But don't be surprised if they buy a new red dress they don't need.

The Hedonist's coping strategy is, to borrow a catchphrase from a couple of sitcom characters, "Treat. Yo. Self."

They are sensory oriented, which means they cater to their eyes, ears, nose, mouth, and touch. They believe that each new pleasurable encounter or acquisition will be the one that finally gives them lasting happiness.

And yet, spoiler alert, it never does.

You can spot a Hedonist by the vertical creases that have formed on their face due to constant disappointment.

They are always let down because they expect to find lasting happiness in the pursuit of pleasure. But pleasure isn't happiness. The pursuit of pleasure only leads one further into the badlands, chasing the next pleasure.

Compared to Nihilists, I don't have as much trash to talk about Hedonists. Their kind hasn't done me wrong that much.

As long as you're not sharing a bank account with one, they're not too bad.

Hedonists don't complain *all* the time. Sometimes their mouths are too full of pastries flown in fresh from Paris.

WORKAHOLISM

The third and final badlands might be the most deceptive.

This is an area you might be encouraged to enter by other people in your life, such as your boss, or the younger humans who will someday inherit your worldly assets.

These badlands are actually a giant treadmill. A hamster wheel for people.

The people who live out here are the ones Dr. Tal Ben-Shahar calls Rat Racers. We also call them Workaholics, or Type A Personalities, or Heart Attacks Waiting to Happen.

Unlike the Nihilist, the Rat Racer hasn't given up on joy. They believe in happiness, and believe that it does exist for them. Unlike the Hedonist, whose pleasures are in the present, the Rat Racer's happiness lies in the future. It's the pot of gold at the end of a rainbow that's always moving just beyond reach.

The Workaholic might even have one of the Hedonist's corny Vision Boards, though her magazine cut-outs will feature wholesome dreams, like Golden Retrievers. There is nothing more wholesome than a Golden Retriever. And one day, when the time is right, the Workaholic will have one. This Golden Retriever's name will be Rascal. Then, and only then, will the Workaholic kick up their little rat feet and enjoy the good life.

For a few hours.

Then they'll get that tickle that they should be working. If they get busy on the hamster wheel, that tickle will go away.

And what's so bad about work? Haven't you heard that productivity is the new piousness? What is life without goals, and deadlines, and quotas, and graphs, and charts? How's a gal supposed to know if she's put in enough solid hours to deserve to feel kinda-sorta okay about herself?

If you're at a social gathering and want to identify the Workaholics, simply yawn and let it slip that you missed several hours of sleep last night because of a deadline. The Workaholics will trip over each other's little rat feet to compete in a contest over who stayed up the latest.

These fools will battle over who slept the least or had to eat the worst food. Whoever suffers most is the winner. The results don't matter nearly as much as the journey. Only the pain of your nose to the grindstone, and endless cups of microwaved coffee will win you the prize of World's Biggest Martyr.

Have some compassion for the Workaholics. Like the others in their badlands, they found a coping mechanism in the mantra of "work harder."

To a person holding a big hammer, every problem looks like a nail.

To the Workaholic, the solution to every problem is to put in more time at the office.

Many become successful, for which they might get labeled as materialist or greedy. Other people resent the Workaholic's success, accusing them of choosing their careers over their family or friends.

But the thing about work is work never accuses you of anything. Work doesn't scream at you over the dinner table that you don't spend enough time with it.

Work is patient.

Work is fair, giving back for everything you put in.

Work is always there for you, any time of day or night.

Come, little rat, and lose yourself in work!

* * *

The thing about the three badlands of unhappiness is they're not entirely bad if you stick in the tourist-friendly area. You can get something positive out of a quick visit. Take in the sights, buy a t-shirt, tip the staff well, but don't sleep with the bartender.

Step into the Nihilist area when your sweet but foolish sister tries to recruit you into her multi-level marketing pyramid that's "different from all the others because the product is actually one you need!" Naw. You've been to this recruitment center before. You know the presentation ends with you taking home a five-hundred-dollar suitcase full of lipstick that smells like cat pee. Tell your sister no, then roll your eyes over how pathetic it is to believe in dreams. Trash talk her to your Nihilist friends, who will all agree.

On a more serious note, it is good to practice letting go of beliefs and dreams that don't serve you. And you definitely should imagine the present moment from the future to get perspective on letting go of the little things that won't matter in the end.

Be a Hedonist when you've been stuck in your head and have all but forgotten you have a body. Pay a stranger to touch your feet so you can remember how much you hate strangers touching your feet. At least you have feet! They're attached to your body. With some healing touch, your consciousness is expanding. You are no longer a floating brain in a jar. You feel much better now, getting in touch with your sensory side. Strawberries taste good. Hot damn! Peel me some grapes, servant.

A little indulgence in sensory pleasure does reduce anxiety. Even those rocks that say BREATHE can help you. Getting a massage or deeply breathing in pleasant scents stimulates the parasympathetic nervous system, which then tells your sympathetic nervous system—the one that gets you wound up—to take a break and relax.

The best time to be a Workaholic is in the past, so you can reap the rewards in the present and future. If you didn't spend time in those badlands in your younger days, you should do a few tours of duty. It'll help your bank account, plus it builds character.

You'll know you're in the Workaholic badlands when you snort at the idea of work-life balance. As if that's a thing! Now chug that Pepto Bismol like the Sweet Pink Milkshake of Success that it is, and get back to work.

* * *

Consider combining these three big coping mechanisms:

- letting go
- treating yourself
- working hard

If you combine these in equal measures, with balance, you should find yourself in the middle of the Venn diagram, standing on the Island of Happiness between the three badlands.

Happiness Island is where you enjoy the present moment, even when it's not perfect. Want to stay here in paradise for as long as possible? It's time to finally start that Gratitude Journal, if you haven't already. Make a list of all the things you already have, that you're truly grateful for. Hey, would you look at that? Your life is pretty sweet.

Now you'll hear a sound, like a tiny bell ringing, off in the distance. Whatever could it be? You clap your hands together in sweet anticipation. Life is good. Good things happen. They're happening all around you, all the time, and all you had to do was avoid the badlands and practice gratitude.

Suddenly, a golden halo falls from the ceiling. How in the holy hell did that get up there? It must be a magic halo. It's floating over your head. You've got the magic in you, baby. Your key to the secret city of Bliss, population you, is in the mail.

In the coming days, you will spontaneously shed five pounds, your boobs will perk up like marshmallow Peeps in the microwave, and you'll never, ever, ever have that recurring dream where you keep opening door after door, unable to find a public washroom with a functioning toilet.

Okay, okay, I was letting my sarcastic Nihilism peek out a little when I was describing happiness.

The truth is, happiness is a great place to be. I can always tell when I'm happy because it's the only time I stop asking myself, *Why am I not happy?*

Happiness is the juncture of three coping strategies working at the same time.

Like the Nihilists, you're able to let go of your attachment to things that aren't useful, such as envy or resentment.

Like the Hedonists, you can slow down to find the pleasures in life, for every storm has an eye, a center of calm.

Like the Workaholics, you understand that good things come to those who help themselves by clocking in.

When life throws garbage your way, you get to choose the coping strategy:

- Take that garbage, fling out your arms, and let it go.
- Hold the garbage to your nose and sniff it deeply, for it might be roses.
- Get to work at your sewing machine, where you turn that garbage into a funky purse you sell at a craft fair.

It's up to you. If you find even more coping strategies than these three, booyeah!

When happiness is working as it should, you might not even know you're there.

P.S. If you think you might be happy, for heavens' sakes, don't go around telling people. One of them is bound to wreck it.

By the same token, when you encounter other happy people, don't be a pickle and ruin it. Don't pick apart their happiness to see how it works, question its validity, or measure it against your own. The world would be a dull place if everyone's happiness looked the same.

If you meet a fellow happy person on your journey, look them in the eye and exchange the secret happy person signal, a smile and a nod, then carry on with your happy ways.

FRENEMIES

I'm at home when I receive a text message from my friend, whom I shall call Hortense Fairweather. (Not her real name.) I had texted Hortense Fairweather earlier that day, casually asking what she'd been up to, since I hadn't seen or talked to her for a while.

Hortense lays into me. "I'm not speaking to you because of what you did to me at the party."

The party?

What I'm staring at is just a text message on my phone, not an attacker with a weapon. But my brain recognizes danger when it comes along. My kidneys compete to see which one can shoot out more panic juice. My mouth goes dry. My peripheral vision is gone. My heart is racing as her words punch me in the gut. *What did I do at the party?*

I don't know what I'm guilty of, but thanks to the sack of shame I haul around most of the time, I am certain that I have done something dreadful.

With shaky hands, I type out a one-size-fits-all blanket apology. Whatever it was I did, I am deeply sorry. I adore Hortense. I feel horrible that she's upset.

Next, I delicately try to determine what it was that I'm apologizing for. I've never felt more like the clichéd dumb husband in a lazy sitcom.

Hortense is apoplectic. She is full of so much rage that it takes several long moments for her next missive to come through. "You know exactly what you did."

Ice water runs through my veins.

I swear to her that I don't know, and offer a lame joke about the number of cocktails consumed at the aforementioned party, which had been ages ago.

Hortense, whom I picture violently jabbing at her phone screen, tells me of my sins in her next messages. According to her, I deliberately humiliated her by mocking her recent publication deal.

That? I almost laugh with relief. Here I thought I'd done something awful. But that? Whatever I said about her book deal, it must have been a mistake, or a dumb joke, or both. If making dumb jokes were a crime, I would be in jail.

I apologize once more, and assure her my intentions had been good.

Nope. My intentions were evil, she says. She knows this because of *how I am*. I'm always saying mean things about other people, including our mutual friend, Frankie Rainclouds. (Not her real name.)

Frankie? She's bringing up my treatment of Frankie?

The thing you need to know about Frankie Rainclouds is that everyone makes fun of her. Everyone. She's that kind of person. You can't be friends with Frankie and not talk about the ridiculous things she does or your head will explode.

How can Hortense be using this against me? Talking trash about Frankie is one of Hortense's favorite pastimes, second only to having unprotected sex with bearded strangers who are old enough to be her father.

But never mind the facts. Hortense's mind has been made up.

In response to my one hundredth apology, Hortense says, "I'm not friends with you anymore."

"We can take a break," I type in, thinking it will just be that.

"It's over," she says in her text message.

But is it really? According to the dots on the screen, she's still typing. I wait.

Then she delivers the death blow. "I don't want to be friends with someone who isn't a good person. And you are not a good person."

Her words hurt. *Not a good person.*

It has been three years since this happened. We haven't talked since. I saw her once in a jeans store, where she pretended not to see me. And she was pregnant. That made it worse. She was going to be someone's mother, which meant someone's mother hated me.

I should have known it would end like this with Hortense. When I look back at how we met, a dramatic breakup seems inevitable.

Hortense and I first crossed paths at an art class. She had signed up with another friend, and Hortense clung to this other woman like they were both pre-teens. Hortense clutched the friend's arm as she giggled at everything the instructor said. My first

111

impression of Hortense Fairweather: possibly high, definitely an idiot.

I kept my distance, until one evening when her giggling buddy wasn't at our art class.

She must have been bored because she came over to me for company. I looked up from my painting, Still Life with Sour Grapes, and saw two big doe eyes and an open, smiling expression. Hortense complimented my painting, saying she envied the confidence in my brush strokes.

At least she has excellent taste, I thought. *Perhaps I rushed to judgment on our first day of class.* There was something *off* about her, but who was I to judge? We've all got our quirks.

What followed was a relationship that ran hot and cold, a relationship that made me question my own sanity. But I stuck with it out of sheer stubbornness. She didn't have many friends, and I didn't want to do what some of her previous friends had done and abandon her for "no reason."

Over time, I would learn that people had good reason to abandon Hortense. For example, her emotional reaction to anything was always a level ten. Plus she needed a lot of male attention. And by "a lot," I mean all of the male attention that exists in the universe. She couldn't handle it if any other female was given attention. Since I am both married and respectable, I didn't throw myself at dudes, which is probably why we lasted as long as we did. Even so, her histrionic drama queen tendencies were an ongoing issue. As was her envy of my life in general.

I'm telling you about Hortense because I think we've all had a Hortense.

Anything we do, Hortense interprets in the worst possible way.

We're late to lunch? It's because we don't respect her time.

We didn't compliment her hair? Obviously we hate her new haircut, or, now that she thinks about it, we've always been envious of her naturally wavy blonde locks, so of course now we can't admit that she looks nice.

I've had more than one Hortense. One of my siblings is a Hortense. The more stable and secure I become in my life, the more I attract these Hortenses.

The worst Hortense I ever had was long ago, and it was a man. A man I dated for far too long.

Once, this man threw a full-on tantrum at me inside a fast food restaurant. He'd asked me to order "the usual" for him while he went to the washroom. When the food arrived, it turned out I had ordered him the wrong burger. While everyone in the restaurant gawked at us, he accused me of ordering my ex-boyfriend's favorite burger because I was still in love with my ex, and probably sleeping with him, too. This Man-Hortense insisted I had ordered the wrong burger because I wanted to hurt him, to throw in his face how little I cared about him and his needs. He threw the burger on the floor, left me in the restaurant, and stormed across the street to purchase cigarettes and alcohol. He would later blame his need to start smoking again on me and all my "thoughtless" actions.

As we drove back to his apartment, he accused me of only being with him because I couldn't find someone better. I sobbed pitifully, letting out the tears I'd been holding since the restaurant. I clutched the handle of the passenger side door and fantasized about hurling myself out into traffic, because at least then it would stop.

I'm so glad that awful day, and the ones on either side of it, belong to the distant past. That relationship is so far out of my life it feels like something that happened to somebody else.

But it did happen to me, and I vowed not to let it happen again. I vowed to be more careful. And I have been careful, but there are always Hortenses around.

There are people in this world who have been hurt, and they don't know how to deal with it except to hurt others. They don't take ownership of their actions, so they have to blame someone else when something goes wrong, or when they feel something they don't like.

Some people will assign malice and bad intentions to things other people do. To things that *you* do. These hurt-but-not-healing people feel free to abuse those around them. They can justify anything.

What has helped me to understand these people is, funnily enough, becoming a writer.

Every great story has a hero, and also a villain, to push the hero into action. For a writer to create a convincing villain, the writer must understand how these villainous people think. The big secret? Villains think like every other person on the planet.

A villain doesn't consider themselves a villain. Villains don't wake up one morning and decide to be a terrible person. Most villains truly believe they are fighting for a good cause, righting some wrong, or bravely avenging some injustice.

In real life, everyone you meet believes they are the hero of their own tale.

Here's what I think happened to my former friend, from her perspective:

Hortense Fairweather, the hero of this story, overhears that bitch Ruby Rey talking shit about Hortense's career.

Ruby Rey, who is a monster, wants people to laugh at Hortense because Ruby Rey is not just a monster but also a garbage person.

Hortense has been feeling self-conscious about her career, poor little lamb, and Ruby Rey should know better than to even bring up the topic. But of course Ruby Rey is inhaling gin and eating up all the attention in the room because she's a notorious attention whore.

Well, not anymore!

Hortense Fairweather kicks that bitch to the curb and never looks back.

The end.

And that, my friends, is every bit as true as my version of events. I was the villain as much as I was the victim, depending on your point of view. When it comes to relationships, and intentions, and all those squishy things we can't see or prove, the truth is very subjective.

Want to avoid being the villain in someone else's story?

There's a certain kind of person you need to watch out for. They will come to you bruised, battered, and friendless, claiming that the whole world is against them. They have the worst luck.

You, however, might be their salvation. At last, a friend they can finally count on. A true friend, unlike all the others, who eventually abandoned them.

If you meet someone like this, be very wary about becoming their salvation, especially if it happens overnight.

Note: Self-awareness doesn't cancel out the danger. Even someone who laughingly points out all of their red flags is still a person with a lot of red flags.

You may already have a Hortense Fairweather. Someone who always assigns the worst intentions to your actions. Someone who sees the world in black and white, and demands that you're either with her or against her. Someone who demands you change your behavior so as not to upset her.

People with these issues need help, and you don't have the training or the consent to give them this help.

You can still show these people compassion and empathy as they battle their demons—nobody's perfect, after all—but you need to understand that at some point you will become the villain in their narrative.

If you're getting into a serious relationship with someone, ask them about their enemies.

Then take a note of how many of these so-called villains started out as friends.

Remember this: *A friend who becomes an enemy has been hating you since the day you met.*

HARD WORK
AND LUCK

I read a lot of memoirs these days. That makes me a statistic. Apparently, as soon as women turn 40, they polish off the leftover birthday cake and trade in all their fiction novels in favor of nonfiction and memoir.

I love books by comedians, actors, writers, and other creative types.

What all of these books have in common is the constant emphasis on hard work. And luck. But mostly hard work. And also luck. Hard work! Luck! HARD WORK! LUCK! You must work hard! And when you fail, which you will, you must know it's due to bad luck!

Think of all the trees that could be saved in the printing of these memoirs if the writers could stop beating this drum. We get it. Most people who are intelligent enough to read a book, understand that success comes to those who work very hard and are prepared when good luck comes along.

As for the small percentage who don't get it, the lazy ones who are only looking for get-rich-quick schemes, these folks aren't going to hear one more lecture about the value of hard work and suddenly grow a work ethic.

That's why I haven't insulted your intelligence by going on about the importance of hard work, and how it leads to luck. You get it.

But I do have a few ideas about hard work that people don't talk about as much.

Here's the big secret: When you're truly interested in some pursuit, the hours you put in don't feel like work. Yes, it feels like time, like hours passing, but it doesn't feel like work.

For example, I spend an hour or more every day reading about news in my industry. This is how I stay on top of things.

When some of my less-focused peers catch a rumor about some big shakeup, they come to me for the scoop. Have I heard about this? Yes. Of course I have. I heard about it last month, when it was actually news.

Whenever a less successful peer comes to me for basic information they should already know, I could chastise them for not putting in the hours to understand their industry. I could put on my Mean Girl Pants and gleefully tear them a new one. But I don't, because I'm not a hypocrite.

The truth is, I only read industry news because *I want to* read industry news.

I take workshops and courses to improve my craft because *I want to.*

I could hand in projects that are simply adequate, and get paid the same amount, but I give all my projects yet another editing pass because *I want to.*

I don't do any of these things because some celebrity memoir, or TED Talk, or fortune cookie told me that in order to succeed, I had to work hard. I put in the hours because I want to.

I hesitate to use the word passionate because it's so overused, especially in the descriptions for bad jobs—seriously, you can measure how terrible and degrading a job is by how many times the word passionate is used in the description—but I truly am passionate about my work.

And here's the second big secret: I also hate my work at times. Hate it with the same level of passion with which I love it.

Every large project includes a low point, usually toward the end, in which I declare that it is my final project, after which I'll quit writing.

Hating your work passionately is not something the big names talk about. But maybe they should.

Hating your work—not constantly, but periodically—is actually a good thing. It keeps you from wandering too far into the badlands of Workaholism. Every time we step away for a break, we gain perspective. When we choose to come back, it's like renewing the vows on our passionate love affair.

Hating your work is like that hole in your bath tub that allows the water to drain out when you get distracted by a phone call and leave the hot water running. It's an emergency overflow pipe. It keeps you from working yourself to death.

The secret to success is not just hard work and luck.

The secret to success is to find some passion for a worthwhile cause, and not let it destroy you.

STOPPED UP

This is the chapter that most sane people would not include in their funny memoir / self-help book.

But this is a fuck-it list book, so I'm going to tell you anyway.

If you become too horrified at any point, please skip ahead to the next chapter.

I've suffered from depression or anxiety for most of my life. And I hated it.

Some people embrace their diagnosis as a part of their identity, but I always felt like depression and anxiety wasn't part of me. I saw myself as a happy person who'd been wrongly trapped inside a sad lump.

I support the movement toward accepting mental illness.

Wait, no. That's not entirely true.

What I do support is the movement toward accepting *people*, however they happen to be. I don't feel so accepting about mental illness. Let's keep fighting it, the way we fight other diseases. Treatment is fine, and some degree of acceptance, but let's not give up on finding cures.

In addition to getting therapy from a nice white-haired lady in a long dress, I have taken a few kinds of medication for my mental health. Not everyone is helped by pills, but I was lucky to have good results. When I got my first prescription, I felt better just holding the slip of paper. There was a bounce in my step as I took my happy little slip of paper to the pharmacy.

My first time on medication, I was like a love-sick fool enjoying a new relationship. I gushed to everyone about my amazing new sweetheart, the pill I took daily. I dosed myself at six o'clock, then spent the evening blissed out with my hobbies. Everything from baking fancy cookies to playing with colored modeling clay was wildly enjoyable.

That's why I'm all for trying medication, under the care and supervision of a qualified medical professional, of course. I've been on and off countless times. Even when I'm not taking it, I like the security of knowing it's available to me as a tool.

The downside of medication, for me, anyway, was the side effects. I got the whole list: weight gain, sex problems, etc. What bothered me the most was the night sweats. Every night, I woke up with soaked sheets. And not from the sex I wasn't having, either. I ruined mattresses with the power of my mighty, overactive sweat glands.

After a while on the medication, I'd accidentally miss my pill for a day and enjoy a dry sleep. That was usually the trigger for me deciding to go off the medication. I would always be hopeful that my underlying issues had resolved, and I wouldn't need to go back on medication again.

But the same issues always came back eventually, so I would apologize to my sweat-stained mattress and go back on the pills again.

All of this changed, however, when I discovered the cure.

The cure!

Now I've got your attention.

It happened by accident, and only after I'd fully accepted my fate to live with my anxiety and depression, and go on and off medication forever.

The happy accident occurred when I'd been off medication and dealing with life rather well. As long as I didn't leave the house, I was fine. Being a writer, this was actually an option for me.

But then, as fate would have it, I had to take some antibiotics for something minor. I didn't think much of it. Two days into the antibiotics, I realized something was gone. Just... gone.

My anxiety was gone.

Suddenly, I could leave the house. I could drive my car, on the freeway, at the full speed limit, without soaking the driver's seat with my fear sweat.

I felt free and joyous, like I had felt on medication, except I wasn't. I was only taking antibiotics.

As all of us do when faced with a medical miracle, I consulted Dr. Google.

No, the internet said, in response to my query. Antibiotics are not a cure for depression. There went that theory.

However, I picked up the trail of something intriguing. I pursued this trail.

Did you know we have neurological tissue in our digestive systems? You may have suspected your stomach has a mind of its own. Surprise, surprise. It actually does.

Your body has a "second brain" that's not inside your head. And no, it's not the "second brain" that runs the squirrel that lives in your pants, you dirty beast.

This second brain is the ENS, or Enteric Nervous System. It's a network of over 100 million nerves that are embedded in the lining of your gastrointestinal system. The ENS is connected to the brain in your skull, and runs from the top of your esophagus all the way to, you know, the bottom. The end of the line. Wink, wink. I'm talking about your b-hole.

The ENS runs from your throat to your anus, and it's all in constant communication with your brain. They are like best friends who finish each other's sentences. How does that work? Like this: When your brain perceives embarrassment happening to you, your ENS finishes the sentence by clenching your anus.

Have you ever called someone a tight ass? Or anal retentive? These descriptions may be more true than you ever imagined.

On some level, you've always understood that your digestion and mind are connected.

When you feel nervous, like before speaking in front of a group, you'll get what we call butterflies in the stomach. If the fear is intense, you might even vomit.

We humans have understood the mind-digestion connection since long before we developed the technology to prove it with science.

Just look at our many metaphors that link mood and digestion:

- I've got a bad feeling in my stomach about this.
- Trust your gut.
- I need time to digest this.
- That awful cashier at Trader Joe's makes me *barf*. I hate her *guts*. Her snide comments have been *eating away* at me. I'm going to *feed her* a knuckle sandwich.

We feel our emotions in our bodies, but what most people don't know, and what I didn't know until recently, is that the connection goes both ways.

For example, an issue in your digestive system can give you anxiety.

Well, duh, you may be thinking. *If I wolf down a big bowl of Curry in a Hurry, I will experience anxiety when the tummy rumbles that tell me to immediately seek a soundproof washroom.*

Yes, tummy-rumble-panic is a good example of the connection, but there are other more subtle ways we are impacted by what's going on down there, inside the thirty-foot-long pipeline that turns food into fuel.

Your digestive system, like other organs, is affected by your overall health. It's also affected by the type, volume, and timing of food you toss in at the top of the pipeline. Constant nibbling plays havoc with your digestive fire. Food intolerances can cause inflammation. Studies have found a correlation between inflammation of the gastrointestinal system and depression.

That's kind of a revelation, don't you think? Inflammation isn't the cause of all depression, but we've found the smoking gun for at least some cases.

You'd think the medical community would make more noise about this, but they don't. I can't blame them too harshly. It's a huge system, strongly influenced by giant pharmaceutical companies who make more profit on treatment than on cures.

You can only sell a cure one time. You can sell a treatment forever.

I used to roll my eyes at the idea of cleanses and special diets. But having my anxiety suddenly clear up like I'd been cured was a big, giant clue I wasn't going to ignore. One side effect of the antibiotics was, as happens to most people, a certain "emptying" of my digestive system. Like a volcano.

In my quest to hold onto my cure, I picked up a bunch of books about the digestive system. I jumped into researching the connection between inflammation, gut bacteria, and mood. The internet isn't the best place to research. Most blog posts that come up under searches belong to entities trying to sell you one product or another. But the truth is out there if you know where to look. What helped me most were not the pretty bloggers and Instagrammers, but the traditionally published books written by professionals with solid credentials.

Soon, I found myself following a program that some might describe as either a cleanse or a special diet. I became a follower of the very things I used to mock. In the writing world, this is what's called a great character arc.

I came to this program after spending a lot of time reading about something called the microbiome. That's the name for the collective DNA of all the single-celled organisms inside our body that don't have human DNA. Of these micro-organisms, the big players are bacteria, but there are also archaea, fungi, viruses, and other microbes.

Inside our digestive system are approximately two pounds of these critters.

You might be thinking, "Ew, yuck! Get these living things that aren't me out of me!"

But you wouldn't want to get rid of your microbiome. These critters are inside us for a reason. In the digestive system, they help us break down food and synthesize the nutrients and hormones we need to survive. Some bacteria help us produce and regulate the mood-enhancing chemicals you may have heard of: dopamine, GABA, and serotonin.

Over the coming years, you'll be hearing a lot more about the microbiome. Not because it's a new fad, but because scientific technology has advanced to the point where we can finally run DNA sequencing on these critters. It's because of the advances in genetic analysis that we're gaining new insight into these hidden worlds within us. Soon, we may have medical treatments that alter our microbiome to prevent disease, allergies, and mood disorders.

Neat. But what about now? What about those of us who don't have DNA sequencing technology, let alone the understanding of what these thousands of different species of micro-organisms do? How do we get this complicated system into a state of balance that enhances our health?

In short, how do we make our microbiome healthy?

That was the task I faced after taking the antibiotics that wiped out the majority of my gut bacteria. I knew I was feeling better thanks to some of the "bad guys" being flushed out, but how was I supposed to get more of the "good guys" to populate my system? I didn't want to return to my previous anxiety-riddled state.

I had a new job. I was going to be the dream landlady for the most desirable tenants. The more I read about digestive health, the more clear it became. I had to do the unthinkable.

I had to eat some kale. Kale and all of its healthy friends. I had to start eating not for my tongue but for my guts.

Once I understood how important vegetable fiber was to my healthy and my mood, I ate the kale. And the other stuff, too. If kale was going to make me happy, then kale was on the menu. How could I not do the best I could to become the ideal landlady for good bacteria?

It was a little harder to avoid the things that fed the bad bacteria, but I was already feeling better. The diet changes seemed to be working, so I stayed on track.

But how did I really know eating kale was worth it? Was it possible my good mood was simply placebo?

What I needed was some sort of physical evidence that my microbiome was getting in better shape.

And this, gentle reader, brings us to the topic of poo.

It also brings us to my newest catchphrase: Fix your poo, fix your mood.

In my quest for better moods, I became an expert on the topic of constipation.

Do you know how many people are chronically constipated and don't even realize it? Let alone how bad it is for them? So many people!

But I'm not constipated, I used to think. I rarely went longer than a day without going. When doctors asked if I was "regular," I would say yes, I was. Regular like clockwork. I would go to the bathroom at the same time every day, right after the first cup of coffee. Isn't that what coffee is for?

I believed my Number Twos were perfectly normal. And, compared to the people around me, including my doctors, my Number Two routine *was* normal, in the sense it was average or typical. But it wasn't healthy.

When your digestive system is properly tuned up, food should be processed relatively quickly and sail out smoothly.

The specific number of hours of "transit time" viewed as ideal will vary by person and health practitioner, so I won't give a number. However, the digestion process should be fast enough that the waste is still pliable and small enough in diameter that it passes without effort. The ideal Number Two looks smooth and bends easily, like a nicely curved banana. Softer is better than firmer.

What you don't want to see your body producing are wide logs with deep cracks. Or, further down the Bristol Stool Chart, the ones that look like a handful of marbles squashed together. The next step is little cannonballs. All these types of Number Two are signs of constipation.

In summary, you want bananas, not cracked logs or squashed marbles or cannonballs. Easy, right?

Don't mind the color too much, as color will vary based on what you've eaten; the texture is the important part.

If you're curious about how long food is in your system, all you need to do is eat a large beet salad. You will notice when that scarlet-hued end product comes out. I love beet salad, so I have this adventure all the time.

After I made the dietary changes to feed my beneficial bacteria, reduce inflammation, and speed up my rate of digestion, my mood picked up even more, and has stayed up.

These days, I'm keenly aware of the connection. I notice how stress causes things to slow down, and how the guts-mood connection goes the other way, as well. A slowdown in transit time due to bad diet choices makes me feel sluggish and mopey.

I can literally eat my way into depression or eat my way out of it. It's my choice.

Do I miss my carefree days of gobbling down garbage without a second thought to my guts? Sure. But I don't miss being depressed and miserable, or anxious and tortured, or having to take medication with bad side effects. And I sure don't miss those regular trips to the furniture store to replace my sweat-soaked mattress.

Listen, I know it's exhausting to deal with all the conflicting health advice you've received over the years.

One minute butter is in, the next minute butter is out, then suddenly it's back in again. The same for eggs, red meat, coconut oil, and so on. If you want an excuse to not eat kale, you can find some study somewhere that declares that kale is the devil and you should only eat chocolate cake.

Your vegetarian friends rave about their supposedly healthy lifestyle. Your vegan friends all want you to go vegan. Your paleo friends want you to go paleo, eat bison heart stew, and join their CrossFit gym. There's a lot of peer pressure to do things that don't look very fun.

On the other hand, there are the food manufacturers. Unlike your peers, these people have deep pockets and a vested interest in what you eat. They use lobbying groups to get what they want. And what do they want? It's not a mystery. Food processors, packagers, and manufacturers want higher profits. They will do anything to keep consumers buying the products that yield the highest profits. They block the proposed legislation designed to regulate their industry.

Back to your peers again. They also have a vested interest in what you eat because they want you to live longer.

But also, they want you to validate their chosen lifestyle. Your friends and family may be helpful or they may not, depending on how much evidence there is behind their choices.

It's hard for individuals like us to battle through all the noise and corporate agendas to find the truth and take control of our health.

For myself, I follow a diet that doesn't have a name. You can call it the Ruby Rey diet. I can't easily explain it to people with one simple word, but, since we've gotten to be such good friends over the course of this book, I can tell you these things about my Ruby Rey diet:

- I get a lot of recipes from paleo websites.
- Daily, I eat two hot meals plus one snack.
- I hold my breath and keep my eyes on my shopping cart when walking past The Gauntlet, which is my name for the bakery counter at my grocery store.

At first, I worried the changes I was making to my diet were going to trigger disordered eating. (I've had some issues with that in the past.)

But, interestingly enough, the exact opposite happened.

When I finally learned which foods were truly beneficial to my body and mind, I realized that my previous disordered eating actually came from the frustration of not knowing more, of not having the answers. Once I had the answers, I had absolute conviction in my healthy choices. No disordered behavior.

Now that I've been following this program for a while, I see a future free of medication. I'm a person who *used to have* depression and anxiety. It's in remission, possibly cured. I am now the happy person I always felt I was.

I also shed those last couple of pounds I'd been trying to get rid of unsuccessfully for years.

If you are looking to shake things up, try making friends with your digestive system.

Sure, your friends will be annoyed when you ask the waitress about the ingredients in the salad dressing. Your family might make fun of you for trying yet another "fad diet" that they don't believe will work. They will, as people do, project onto you their own learned helplessness.

Fuck it.

Fix your poo, fix your mood.

WE ARE ALL
WATCHING
OURSELVES IN
THE MOVIE
OF OUR LIVES

I'm not in a book club. I'm in *two* book clubs. Both of them are constantly in danger of being put on my fuck-it list.

The best thing about any club is the people; the worst thing about any club is the people.

When a meeting goes well, it's wonderful. People share, bond, laugh, and love. I can leave gatherings with an invigorated feeling that lasts for days.

And then there are the meetings that don't quite come together. Sometimes it's due to one bad apple. Other times, the lack of leadership is to blame. In the void that comes with a lack of direction, people who are normally constructive can easily become destructive.

One of my book clubs is running more smoothly these days, ever since I stepped up to help organize. The group had been on an indefinite "break" for about a year when I recently decided to give it the ol' kick in the pants to get going again.

Flashback to three months ago:

I post a cheery announcement that the book club is starting back up again. Our first meeting of the year will be this Monday. Yay! Balloons and streamers, etc.

The very first response I get is an email from a woman who has a few complaints. She doesn't have an issue with me leading the meeting, but she does have an issue with the date, the topic, and the venue.

I am anything but surprised. This isn't my first rodeo, folks. I've tried and failed to be a club leader multiple times, and I've learned things the hard way.

If you ever find yourself in a leadership position, you will discover the following:

1. The less money people pay for something, the less they value it; free events always attract more belly-achers.
2. Destructive people believe that tearing down or picking apart what others are doing has just as much value as being constructive and helping.
3. One in five attendees believes the meeting is all about them. Just kidding. It's one in three.

When I receive this woman's email complaining about the date, topic, and venue, I take a moment to breathe, compose myself, and reply.

As much as I'd like to tell her to go pound sand, I do *not* tell her to go pound sand.

I thank her for the feedback, and promise I will keep an eye open for other options.

This lady has no idea that the group has been on hiatus due to the endless complaining from people like her. The previous organizers tried to make everyone happy. They kept changing nights and venues, but could never get it perfect. They let the negativity bring them to their knees.

If you've never been in a leadership role before, you might be shocked by how ineffective people are at teamwork. People who are supposedly there to support an endeavor try instead to halt progress at every turn. And these are people at a fun group, for fun! Can you imagine what hellspawn troublemakers they are at their workplaces?

People who are destructive instead of constructive have a variety of tactics. Some demand that every organizational detail be locked down and decided *yesterday*, while others insist on keeping all options open *for all eternity*. People will pout about not being listened to, and then go on to interrupt everyone else. Everyone has an agenda, and everyone's agenda is different. By law, every book club contains at least one person who came there to drink, to complain, to start a fight, or all of the above.

Being a leader can be a thankless task, like herding cats, but I'm going to keep doing it. Even in the face of whining, and gossiping, and undermining —some of it not even my own!—I will keep stepping up as a constructive force. There are two reasons.

1. Despite being an introvert, I do enjoy having some occasion to put on pants, step outside, and socialize with other humans.
2. All groups need leaders. I can be proud of myself for stepping up, even when it means

taking some shit. Now, I realize it's just a book club, and I'm not saving the world, or solving the energy crisis, or curing stubborn foot fungus, but I choose to help others and be in service of my community. In doing so, I get more out of the deal than I'm putting in. By volunteering, I get to feel good about myself.

That last point is a biggie, so I'll repeat it.
By volunteering, I get to feel good about myself.
Here's the thing:
If you have low self-esteem and want to change it, you can't simply decide to suddenly stop believing you're a garbage person. Nothing you do solely in your head is going to fix your self image. You have to go forth into the world, physically and bodily, and do something positive.

You don't have to save the world, either. Think small. Haven't you ever gotten a buzz simply from holding a door open for someone?

I've learned a lot about how to be a happier human, thanks to being a writer.

The biggest lesson of all came from understanding that all movie watchers decide how good or bad a character in a movie is by watching them in action.

If I write a main character who doesn't interact positively with at least one person early in the story, or do something meaningful for others, no audience is going to care what happens next, let alone fall in love with that character.

However, if I write a fictional character who forces herself to smile, and be kind to people, even though it takes effort, and other people have terrible breath and worse manners, the audience will love that character, because she is Bridget Jones, and everyone loves Bridget Jones.

Here's where I blow your mind.

We are all constantly watching ourselves in the movie of our lives. And we are judging ourselves the exact same way we judge people in movies.

We make up our minds about who *we* are as people based on what we see ourselves doing.

It's really that simple. It's about physical, observable actions in the real world. Not our thoughts. You can't see thoughts in a movie. Only actions.

You may be aware of your thoughts, but what you observe yourself doing in the physical world means so much more than any thought, intention, or mantra.

Did you know that you, too, can be as lovable as Bridget Jones? Yes, you.

To increase your worth as a human being, do things that only worthy humans do. As you observe yourself in action being a leader, or a helper, or a nice friend, you'll see yourself more clearly as the good person you are.

Want to say goodbye to feeling like a garbage person? Remember that thoughts and intentions are not quite enough. You must put your feet into the world. Do stuff.

Here's how to bring out your inner lovable rom-com heroine:

1. Listen to other people, even if they're boring. Spoiler alert: most people are boring, but that's okay, because so are you. (Not to me. I think you're amazing.)
2. Give generously to those who'll never repay you. If you're only giving to people you know

will pay you back, that's not giving. It's lending, which is not the same as giving. Note that this doesn't mean you have to become a doormat. If you're asked to give too much, you can politely say no, but at least be the sort of person who considers it. There are many ways to give. Money is obvious, but there's also time, energy, compassion, understanding, patience, and so forth.

3. Believe that everyone you meet is trying their hardest, even when their supposed best efforts yield results that are objectively terrible.

4. Be kind to everyone, even those who don't deserve it. *Especially* to those who don't deserve it. It's very easy to be nice to nice people who deserve niceness. The true test of your inner goodness comes when you're dealing with those who are difficult. So what if they don't "deserve" it? If every act of kindness builds up your kindness muscles, you're getting back more than you're giving.

5. Never do anything you can't discuss after dinner.

6. Don't run over people with your golf cart.

If you do good things regularly, and don't run over people with your golf cart, your self esteem will rise, guaranteed. You will also gain the ability to recognize the good in other people.

Practicing goodness is like learning how to speak another language. Once you're fluent, you'll hear it, see it, and feel it everywhere. Isn't it better to live in a world where goodness is all around?

You've only got one life to live. Don't spend it learning how to be a dick.

When my dick qualities pop up, as they do when I'm rubbed the wrong way (tee hee), I accept the negativity for what it is: Thoughts. Emotions. Passing energy.

Just because I experience some internal negativity, it doesn't define who I am. Besides, studies have shown that negativity is quite high in people with critical thinking skills. It's part of what makes us smart.

It's not wrong to experience negativity, so don't beat yourself up. Let those feelings pass through like bad weather. You can't control the weather, and you can't control everything you feel.

What you do have control over is what you do in the physical world, your actions and words—everything you can observe in the movie you're always watching, starring you.

Though it's tempting to get down in the mud of negativity, you must not give in. Oh, that drama-llama kibble looks delicious, and the first bites are so addictive, but where will it leave you? The drama will pass, and you'll be one sad, bloated, hungover llama. And all the other llamas will be giving you the hairy eyeball. If you were so quick to get down in the mud with one of the other llamas, who will you turn on next?

Say no to the drama llamas and their vicious, empty-calorie lives.

Instead, look within yourself for the wrinkled and wise benevolent elder who came with your soul. Find your inner crone and ask for her crone wisdom. It might take a minute. Crones cannot be rushed. Old bones, dearie. Old bones.

It might help to close your eyes and hold one hand over your heart, where she lives.

Listen to your inner crone of wisdom. She'll advise you to take the high road.

Listen to that old broad, and always, always, always choose the high road.

If you find yourself laboring over some big decision, and you keep asking more and more people for their advice, it's because you're looking for someone to give you permission to do the wrong thing. Don't do the wrong thing. Stop grubbing around for permission, and just do the right thing.

Be a lovable main character.

Be above the drama llamas.

Be a leader. Even if it's just for yourself.

THE END
IS THE
BEGINNING

I am sitting in a warm, steamy Vietnamese restaurant. The place has mustard yellow walls and too many mirrors facing each other, reflecting into infinity. I feel like I'm inside that weird multi-dimensional thing at the end of *Interstellar*. The tesseract, or hypercube.

A waiter comes to take my order, but I need five more minutes. He returns in two. I'm stressed, and my brain isn't working. The menu is a blur of squiggles. I ask for another five minutes. He goes, then returns immediately. This must be Einstein's Theory of Relativity in action. Time for me versus time for the waiter is moving at very different rates.

I begin, "I'll have the..." I trail off.

He is already putting a steaming bowl of wonton soup in front of me. He must have traveled through a wormhole. He created a world-ripping paradox, in order to bring me my soup even before I've asked for it.

I mutter my gratitude and dip the ceramic spoon into the broth. It tastes like warm bath water. There must be other flavors, and salt, but my tongue and brain report only that the broth is a safe temperature to ingest.

Intense stress causes us to temporarily lose some of our senses, including smell and taste. Loud noises have a similar effect, which is why the meals served on airplanes are heavily salted. Airline food doesn't taste that great in the air, but it would be inedible back on the ground in a quiet room.

Gradually, with each slurp of wonton soup, my sense of taste returns, and I mull over my day. I won't get into the details here, because they don't matter. We all have rough days. Mine was one of those. People cried. I feel anger as I mentally break down what happened, and assign blame to the guilty or incompetent parties.

But by the final spoonfuls of soup, I'm no longer upset. I've been hard at work reframing my day. I've been changing labels.

Today is no longer THE VERY BAD DAY THAT UNFAIR THINGS HAPPENED TO ME.

It is THE BAD DAY OTHER PEOPLE CRIED BUT I TRIUMPHANTLY DID NOT.

And, when I really think about it, it's actually THE BAD DAY I SAILED THROUGH WITH DIGNITY, AND HUMOR, AND PROFESSIONALISM, BECAUSE I AM A BOSS.

Or, going further still, it could be called ONE OF THOSE DAYS I LEARNED HOW FUCKING BADASS I CAN BE IN THE FACE OF ADVERSITY.

Ladies and gentlemen, I'm please to report that, after paying my bill and tipping generously, I left that restaurant with a tummy full of soup and a heart full of joy. I may have walked in a loser, but I marched out a winner.

Remember a few chapters back when I said we don't have control over our emotions? We don't, at least not in the white-hot moment of motivating stimulus. For example, when the bad shit was going down earlier that day, I wasn't feeling any positive emotions. And that's okay. Despite the fear, anger, and frustration, I still kept control over my actions and behaved according to my personal rules of conduct. It's all anyone can hope to do.

But we do have control over our emotions sometimes. There is a way we can use our thoughts to help guide how we are feeling.

While I was eating soup, quietly and alone with my thoughts, that was when I regained control.

Through years of practice, countless hours of working to see the good in every situation, it's become second nature for me to find a positive way to view things that happen. Sometimes it takes a while to get to the point where I can put a good label on a bad event. It can take hours, days, or years.

Other times, I surprise myself and see the good while the bad is actually still happening.

It is hard to be in your rational mind when your emotional center is being flooded by stimulus, but the more you practice, the better you'll get.

This might be what some people mean when they say they "choose to be happy." Maybe these annoying people aren't Happiness Assholes after all. They just leave out a few crucial steps because their habits are so ingrained they aren't aware of them anymore.

Why should you learn how to reframe your memories? Because it improves your future.

A good way to feel optimistic about the future is to view the past in a positive way. That doesn't mean changing your memories, just reframing them.

Speaking of which, did you know that none of your memories are the truth?

Not a single one.

Your mind is nothing like a data storage drive or a roll of camera film. Your memories are much closer to finger paintings than they are to photographs. Nothing in there is objective. It's all subjective.

That's why eyewitness testimony is never as strong in a court case as physical evidence. And that's why there are no reputable scientific papers that use eyewitness testimony to prove a theory.

Our memory is inaccurate because it has to be. We take in so much input, every minute of every day. It's too much to store. If we didn't filter, compress, or forget, we'd be in big trouble.

With perfect recall, we'd arrive for work on Monday morning, get asked about our weekend, then have to sift through the raw memories, all forty-eight hours' worth, to review the data for judgment. It would be Wednesday by the time our coworkers got the answer that our weekend was "fine."

In order to remember our lives, we have to simplify and compress our experiences.

Whether we realize it or not, we are always applying labels, too.

These labeled experiences become our stories.

The stories we tell others.

The stories we tell ourselves.

Whenever we have a rough day that leaves us feeling bad, we can:

- Complain endlessly.
- Eat chocolate and drink wine until everything gets blurry.
- Hide from our thoughts by watching television or playing video games.
- Act like a garbage person and create new drama as a distraction.
- Pass the bad mood on to someone else by making them feel worse than we do.
- Accept defeat and sob under a blanket.
- Plot vengeance.

Or we can:

- Find a way to make ourselves the hero who learned something during this recent adventure.

Your gal, Ruby Rey, is far from perfect. She might cycle through three, four, or every one of the bad choices on her way to the good choice. But she's going to keep trying until she gets there.

If she can do it, so can you.

* * *

So, hey, we're nearing the end of this book.

I'd love to stick around and talk to you forever, but I need to get back to my main gig. And I think I've given you plenty to think about until we meet again.

We've talked about how being born of assholes and raised by assholes doesn't mean a person can't do better for themselves, escaping the family curse.

I was eventually able to fix myself, but trust me, your girl screwed up plenty along the way. My late teens and early twenties were a horror show. But there was always something I felt connected to, something that pulled me through those years. What saved me was a thread of hope that felt like a rope I could hang onto, that kept me moving toward the light.

Some folks might say this safety rope was a higher being. I would never say it wasn't. But to me, this thread felt like it was a ray of light coming back through time from this moment, the one happening now.

Somehow, like that tesseract in Interstellar, the Ruby Rey of the future, perhaps Ruby in her mid-forties, or the 90-year-old crone version, or an infinite number of potential older versions, was connected to the younger one in the past. Whenever I hit a new low in my early twenties, I swear I could feel myself in the future, calling back encouragement. Telling me to quit smoking, give up my bad lifestyle, and get my ass back on track, back on the good path. That bright pull from the future was guiding my hand every time I made a better choice.

It hasn't been easy for me. Between having a face for radio, carrying this chip on my shoulder, and always acting too damn brainy (or insufferable) to be universally liked, this path of mine has been uphill and through bad terrain.

But I've seen beautiful sights, too. Sunrises, forests, and oceans. Clean sheets on a freshly-made bed. My wedding day. The faces of my friends as I hold their new babies and they chastise me for not having washed my hands with antibacterial soap.

Another birthday is just around the corner. I'll be forty-five.

Sometimes I hope I've learned everything I need to know, so that life can take it easy on me for a while. But I know that isn't going to happen. The next forty-five years will be filled with new challenges. Hell, the next week will contain at least one event that will threaten my super chill, fuck-it attitude.

How about you?

Have the years you've lived been easy on you?

Or have they been your greatest teacher?

If you were to write a book like this, or send a message back in time to your younger self, what would you say?

Or, if you were to send a message to yourself in the future, what would it be?

Go. That's something you can do.

Go, and get a piece of scrap paper, or a Post-It note, or a grocery receipt, and write something to your future self. Grab a felt pen and write it on your hand if you like.

If you don't know how to start, feel free to use this as a template:

Dear Tomorrow Me:
First of all, I love you. I see how hard you've been trying, and I appreciate everything you do, even if I don't always recognize the good things while

149

you're doing them. I swear I'm going to get better at celebrating achievements, no matter how small.

Second, we're almost out of coffee. So, like, if you happen to go by the store...

Third, it's time to make a couple of changes. Nothing huge and dramatic. But our pal Ruby Rey has some good tips about communicating with our inner crone of wisdom. Is that what she was called? The crone is supposed to be us, but in the future, right? I got a little distracted by the time-traveling waiter with the wonton soup. Anyway, I think it's a fun idea to become a better listener, to other people and to ourselves. Also, there are a couple of things we've been avoiding, and it might be time to make a move. Just thinking about it gives me goosebumps!

So, how do you feel about kale?

We can talk later. No need to tackle everything at once.

XOXO, Past You

Made in the USA
Coppell, TX
19 November 2021

66009175R00085